Minecraft®
Modding For Kids

FOR DUMMIES®
A Wiley Brand

Minecraft®
Modding For Kids

FOR DUMMIES®
A Wiley Brand

by Sarah Guthals, Ph.D
Stephen Foster, Ph.D
Lindsey Handley, Ph.D

FOR DUMMIES®
A Wiley Brand

Minecraft® Modding For Kids For Dummies®

Published by **John Wiley & Sons, Inc.,** 111 River Street, Hoboken, NJ 07030-5774, www.wiley.com

Copyright © 2015 by John Wiley & Sons, Inc., Hoboken, New Jersey

Published simultaneously in Canada

For general information on our other products and services, please contact our Customer Care Department within the U.S. at 877-762-2974, outside the U.S. at 317-572-3993, or fax 317-572-4002. For technical support, please visit www.wiley.com/techsupport.

Wiley publishes in a variety of print and electronic formats and by print-on-demand. Some material included with standard print versions of this book may not be included in e-books or in print-on-demand. If this book refers to media such as a CD or DVD that is not included in the version you purchased, you may download this material at http://booksupport.wiley.com. For more information about Wiley products, visit www.wiley.com.

Library of Congress Control Number: 2015940558

ISBN: 978-1-119-05004-9; ISBN: 978-1-119-05765-9 (ePDF); ISBN: 978-1-119-05767-3 (ePub)

Manufactured in the United States of America

10 9 8 7 6 5 4

Contents at a Glance

Table of Contents

Introduction

So you want to *mod Minecraft* — that's a great idea! You're about to be transformed from a Minecraft player into a Minecraft maker, and in order to get there, you have to learn how to code. The task is quite simple, because you'll use many of the skills you already have — logic, creativity, math, gaming, and problem solving — to design, build, test, and share Minecraft mods. This book tells you everything, from building a large house to making a multiplayer game that you can play *inside* Minecraft with your friends.

About This Book

Minecraft modding used to be a task that only expert coders could take on. And becoming an expert coder was no easy task, because that topic is rarely taught in school. Luckily, the information in this book shows you how to be a coder *and* how to be a Minecraft modder. Like content across the entire *For Dummies* series, this book is clearly written, fun to read, and organized in an easy-access format. By using your new skills, you can be well on your way to coding successfully in other applications and transforming the way you and your friends play Minecraft.

Modding Minecraft For Kids For Dummies is assembled as a series of mods that feature steps for designing, building, and testing each mod, from start to finish. As you work through each project, keep a couple of conventions in mind:

Programming code and web addresses appear in monofont. If you're reading a digital version of this book on a device connected to the Internet, note that you can click web addresses to visit that website, like this: www.dummies.com.

Working with LearnToMod is super simple: I generally just give you instructions such as "Drag a function into the programming environment" or "Click on the Minecraft category and then Players." Or I may simply tell you to click on a link or a tab.

Foolish Assumptions

In this book, I make a few assumptions about you in regard to getting started:

✔ You're reasonably comfortable typing on a computer and using a mouse. Your experience can be on a Windows system or a Mac system; either one will do. All coding takes place in a web browser — and on any browser on either platform. The figures in this book show LearnToMod operating on a Mac using the Chrome browser.

✔ You're capable of navigating a standard website, because LearnToMod takes place only in your web browser.

Furthermore, I've made some assumptions with regard to your entrance into the world of Minecraft modding:

✔ You have played Minecraft, and you understand the basic mechanics of playing. Regardless of whether you play Minecraft on Windows or the Mac, you must use the desktop version. The Pocket Edition, which is played on mobile devices, doesn't work with LearnToMod.

✔ You're comfortable with basic math principles, math operations such as adding whole numbers, and logical operations such as comparing two whole numbers.

Icons Used in This Book

The Tip icon marks advice and shortcuts that you can use to make modding easier.

The Remember icon marks concepts you should keep in mind to make modding easier.

The Coding Connections icon describes how the modding you're doing relates to the bigger picture of coding.

The Math Connections icon describes math that is being used in your modding.

Watch out! This icon marks important information that may save you from the common headaches that modders sometimes have to endure.

Accessing the LearnToMod Software

To access the LearnToMod software, you use the access key located on the inside front cover of this book. Then all you need to do is follow these steps to access your new LearnToMod account:

1. **Go to** http://mod.learntomod.com.

   The first time you log in, the site redirects you to ThoughtSTEM's login page to create your account.

2. **Use the Sign Up window (located below the Log In window) to create your LearnToMod account.**

   If you need to, you can contact the LearnToMod customer service team at learntomod@thoughtstem.com.

You can choose whatever password you want for your account. It does *not* have to be the access key.

3. **After you create your LearnToMod account, you are redirected to a page that asks for your access key. Copy and paste the access key that appears in the inside front cover of this book.**

4. **Choose a LearnToMod nickname — any name you want!**

You see the dashboard (the Home screen). Now you can start unlocking badges to learn how to mod!

Obtaining an Access Key as an E-Book Reader

E-book readers must answer a security question to receive an access key for the LearnToMod software trial.

1. **Go to** `http://www.dummies.com/go/getaccess`.

You see a welcome message and a drop down menu, "Select Your E-Book."

2. **Use the drop down menu to choose Minecraft Modding For Kids For Dummies.**

If you need to, you can contact the Dummies customer service team at `http://dummies.custhelp.com`.

3. **Complete the registration page.**

Answer the security code at the bottom of the page to receive the e-mail with your access key.

4. **Follow the instructions provided in the Accessing the LearntoMod Software section of this chapter to access the free trial.**

   If you need to, you can contact the LearnToMod customer service team at learntomod@thoughtstem.com.

Beyond the Book

I'm making available some extra content that you won't find in this book. Go online to find these items:

✔ **An online Cheat Sheet for LearnToMod and basic Minecraft modding is available at** www.dummies.com/cheatsheet/minecraftmoddingforkids. The description of basic modding skills that's condensed into the Cheat Sheet shows the fundamentals of mod design and coding.

✔ **Online articles covering additional topics are available at** www.dummies.com/extras/minecraftmoddingforkids.

✔ **You can find updates to this book, if they become necessary, at** www.dummies.com/updates/minecraftmoddingforkids.

Where to Go from Here

LearnToMod was developed to guide students just like you through the challenges of Minecraft modding, to present coding concepts and demonstrate how much fun it can be to start making fun and exciting Minecraft mods. LearnToMod has over 200 badges that guide you in the creation of simple mods; however, you can also make your own creative mods. If you need guidance in making larger, more creative mods, we aren't in the same physical location for me to show you how, so I show you how to make these larger, more creative mods using a method that has worked well for hundreds of *For Dummies* books: This book uses printed instructions and screen shot examples to guide you through a series of fun projects!

The mods in the earlier chapters of this book are pretty simple to complete, but later mods are larger, more complex, and more difficult. The mods are intended to be completed sequentially, and sometimes they build on each other — but you're welcome to jump around and try out harder projects first.

After you have made a few Minecraft mods with the help of this book, millions of mods are waiting for you to write them. You can go to the LearnToMod site and continue earning badges, or continue creating and sharing mods with other LearnToMod modders. Even more, you're learning how to code! You can also go out and find other languages and applications in which to code. Coding is exciting, and I'm glad that you have chosen to not only learn to code but also transform the way you and your friends play Minecraft!

Part 1
Making Your First Minecraft Mod

This week you'll:

Getting Started on Modding Minecraft

In this book, I show you how to write minigame Minecraft mods. A *minigame* Minecraft mod is a game that you play *inside* of Minecraft. You can see how to make several minigames and gain the skills you need to perfect a minigame of your own creation.

The LearnToMod online software teaches you how to make modifications, or *mods,* that you can run in the multiplayer version of Minecraft. With hundreds of badges to guide you through various programming concepts and mods, you'll gain the skills necessary to make creative mods of your own. You should have some basic familiarity with playing Minecraft, but you don't need to be an expert. All you need is the computer version of Minecraft and an Internet connection.

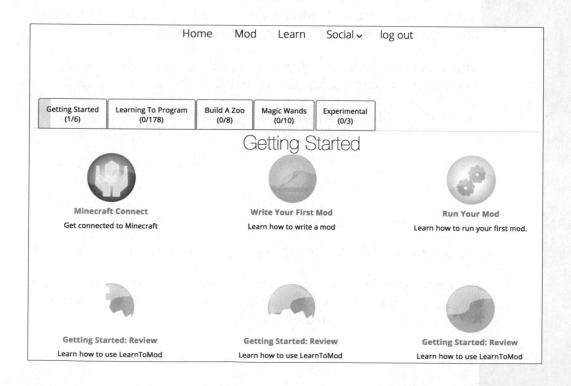

In this chapter, I explain what a mod is, describe how to use the LearnToMod online software and how to connect to the LearnToMod multiplayer Minecraft Server, and spell out how to use the basic tools, such as invisible robots, that you need in order to make your own, fun-filled mods.

Know What Minecraft Modding Is

Video games are made up of thousands of lines of code. Code makes players (like you) able to explore new worlds, interact with characters, and have fun.

Some games, like Minecraft, allow players to add their own code to the games to create new worlds, challenges, or even characters. Throughout this book, I show you how to write these game modifications — or *mods* — and you can then see how to write code.

Perhaps you have already begun to explore the world of Minecraft mods. Programmers all around the world have created their own mods and then shared them with Minecraft players — for free.

Mods can consist of almost any task; this list describes a few tasks that you can accomplish by using mods:

- **Texture:** Change the way the Minecraft world looks by applying a new texture pack.

- **Block interaction:** Cause an explosion whenever the player destroys a block of type wood.

- **New block:** Create new blocks.

- **Minigame:** Create a minigame to play *within* a Minecraft world.

- **Large structure:** Create huge structures to explore and personalize — ones that would take a long time to make by hand but take only a short time to make with code.

Use the LearnToMod Online Software

The LearnToMod online software walks you through a series of challenges that you complete in order to earn badges. These challenges help show you basic programming skills and how to make Minecraft mods.

In this section, I show you how to log in to the LearnToMod online software (available at `mod.learntomod.com`), create and run your first mod, and share that mod with other modders.

Sign up for the LearnToMod online software

Signing up for the LearnToMod online software is quick and easy. It takes only about 5 minutes to complete the sign-up process and start earning badges.

Find your access key for LearnToMod on the inside front cover of this book, and then follow these steps to access your new LearnToMod account:

1. **Go to** `http://mod.learntomod.com`.

   The first time you log in, the site redirects you to ThoughtSTEM's login page to create your account.

2. **Use the Sign Up window (located below the Log In window, as shown in Figure 1-1) to create your LearnToMod account.**

   If you need to, you can contact the LearnToMod customer service team at learntomod@thoughtstem.com.

   You can choose whatever password you want for your account. It does *not* have to be the access key.

3. **After you create your LearnToMod account, you are redirected to a page that asks for your access key. Copy and paste the access key that appears in the inside front cover of this book, as shown in Figure 1-2.**

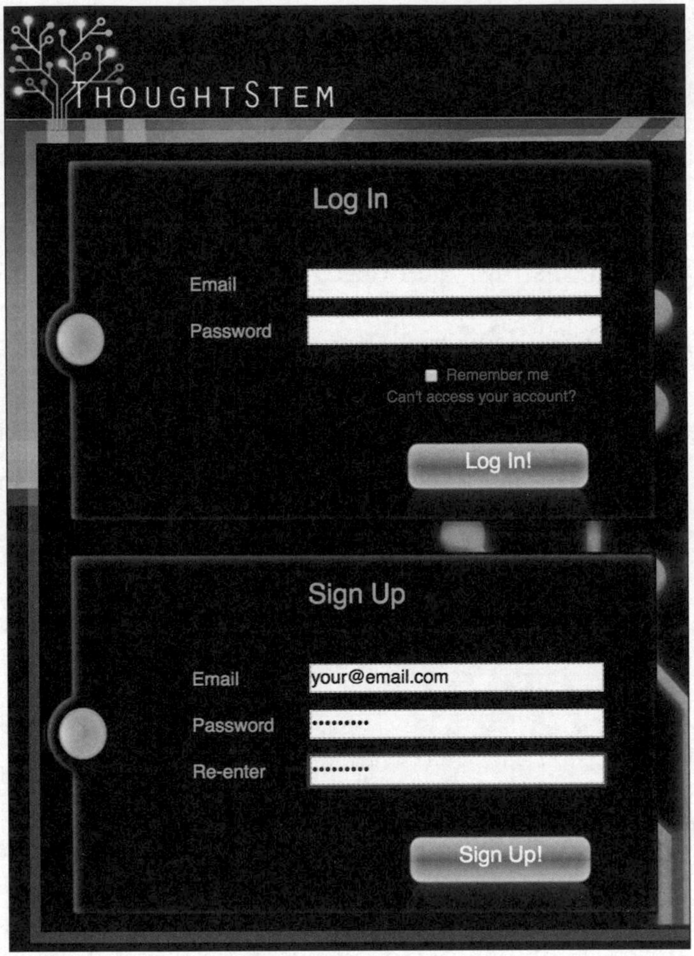
THOUGHTSTEM
Log In
Email
Password
Remember me
Can't access your account?
Log In!
Sign Up
Email
your@email.com
Password
Re-enter
Sign Up!

Figure 1-1

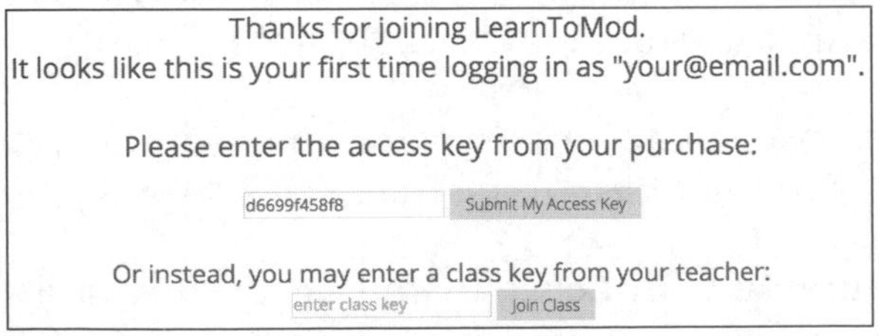
Thanks for joining LearnToMod.
It looks like this is your first time logging in as "your@email.com".
Please enter the access key from your purchase:
d6699f458f8
Submit My Access Key
Or instead, you may enter a class key from your teacher:
enter class key
Join Class

Figure 1-2

4. **Choose a LearnToMod nickname (see Figure 1-3). Pick any name you want!**

You see the dashboard (the Home screen), as shown in Figure 1-4. Now you can start unlocking badges to learn how to mod!

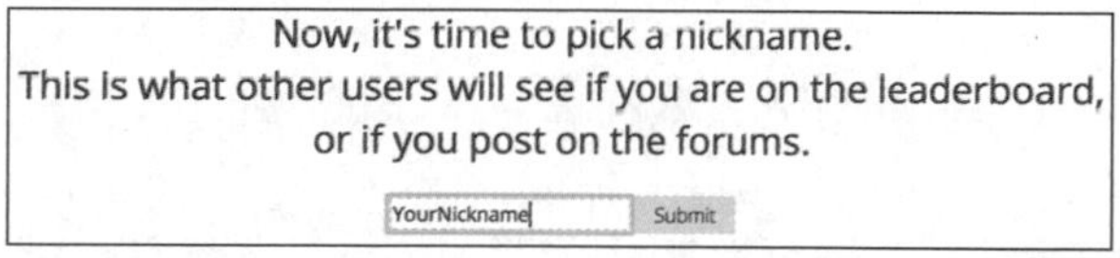

Now, it's time to pick a nickname.
This is what other users will see if you are on the leaderboard, or if you post on the forums.

YourNickname   Submit

Figure 1-3

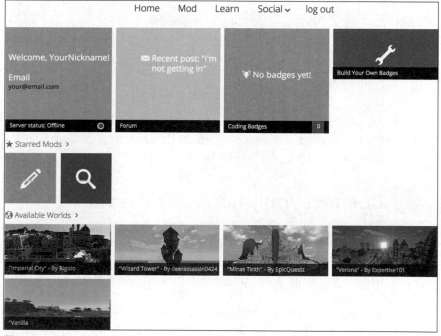

Figure 1-4

Get started with the LearnToMod badges

To access your LearnToMod badges, log in at `http://mod.learntomod.com` with the email address and password you used to sign up (refer to Figure 1-1). You see the home page (refer to Figure 1-4). To see the list of challenges, click on the Learn tab at the top of the home page. You see the first set of challenges, as shown in Figure 1-5.

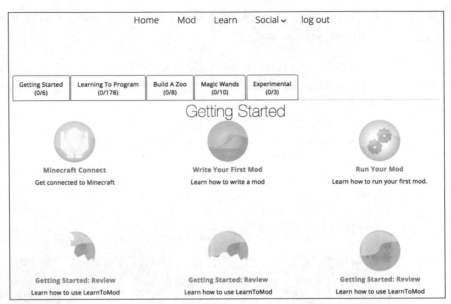

Figure 1-5

As you complete challenges, color is added to the badges so that they no longer appear shaded. Badges that are shaded, like those in Figure 1-5, have yet to be earned.

Connect your mods to Minecraft

To get started, click on the first badge, Minecraft Connect. In this badge, you can find all the instructions to help you connect your mods to Minecraft so that you can see their effects in the game. In this section, I summarize those steps for you.

To run your mods in Minecraft, you should have the most recent version of Minecraft. Over time, Minecraft improves by way of updates, and you should always use the newest version so that you have access to the newest LearnToMod features. To see which version of Minecraft you're running, follow these steps:

1. Click the Edit Profile button in the lower left corner of the Minecraft startup screen, shown in Figure 1-6.

2. In the Profile Name text box, name the new profile (see Figure 1-7).

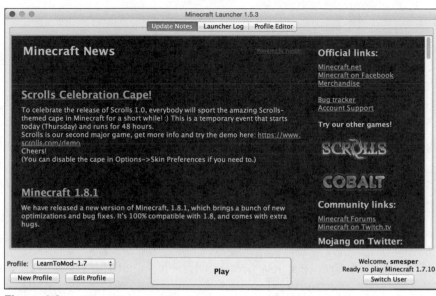

Figure 1-6

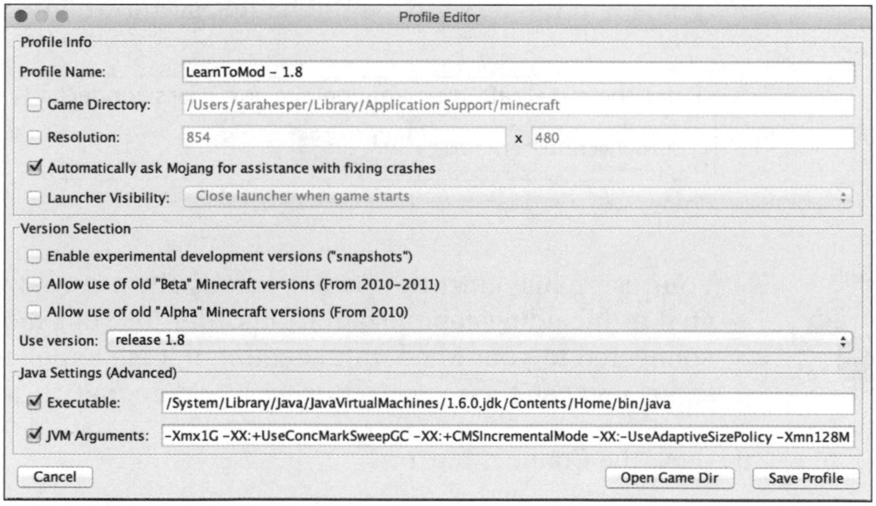

Figure 1-7

3. Look at the Version Selection section, shown in Figure 1-8, to see which version you're using. It's in the Use Version text box. You should be using the version at the top of the list. In this case, it's version 1.8.

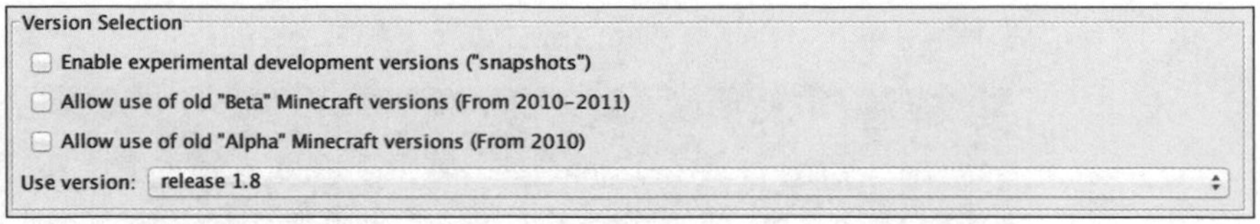

Figure 1-8

4. Click the Save Profile button at the bottom of the screen (refer to Figure 1-7).

   If you're using an earlier version (such as version 1.7), you should complete one of these actions:

   • Change it to the most recent version.

   • Create a new profile where you set the version to the most recent version.

5. Add your Minecraft username to the LearnToMod account by typing it in the text box on the badge, as shown in Figure 1-9.

Enter the minecraft username below, and press connect.

| YourMinecraftUsername | Connect |

Figure 1-9

Your username must be spelled exactly the same as you created it (including capitalization) in order for your mods to be connected to your Minecraft account. If it isn't spelled the same, you can't see your mods within Minecraft.

6. Click the Connect button.

   The Minecraft Connect badge pops up, as shown in Figure 1-10.

   Under the text box in the Minecraft Connect badge, you see the text `Success!`, as shown in Figure 1-11.

Follow the 11 steps that you see onscreen in the Minecraft Connect badge:

Figure 1-10

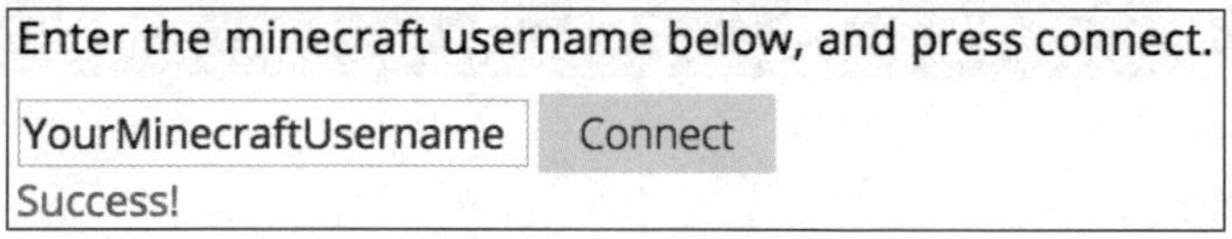

Enter the minecraft username below, and press connect.

| YourMinecraftUsername | Connect |

Success!

Figure 1-11

1. Click Play on the Minecraft home screen (refer to Figure 1-6).

2. Choose Multiplayer.

3. Click Add Server.

4. Type **Learn To Mod** as the server name, and type **play.learntomod.com** as the server address.

5. Click Done.

6. Click Join Server.

When you have completed these steps, you see a prebuilt world that looks similar to the one shown in Figure 1-12. It's similar to a waiting room. You can explore this world while Minecraft finds you a new world in which you can test your mods. Your wait time should be between 1 and 5 minutes. (Be patient — it's not that long!)

If you're having trouble connecting to the LearnToMod server, email the technical support team at learntomod@thoughtstem.com.

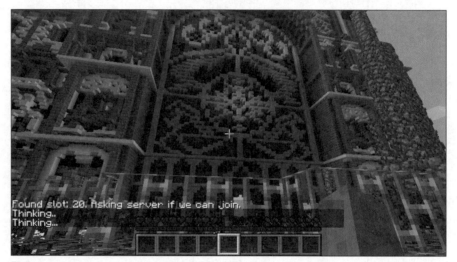

Figure 1-12

Whenever you're connected to your testing world, you have a mod chest in your inventory (see the bottom of Figure 1-13), and you can play in either Creative mode or Survival mode.

Figure 1-13

Become Familiar with the Programming Environment

Before you begin your modding adventure, you should be familiar with the programming environment you'll use.

1. Click the Learn tab at the top of the LearnToMod website.

   You're taken to the first set of challenges again, as shown in Figure 1-14.

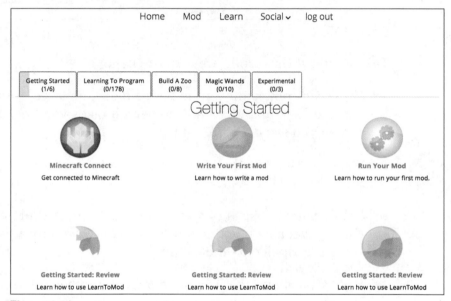

Figure 1-14

2. Click the Write Your First Mod badge.

   You see the challenge (see Figure 1-15).

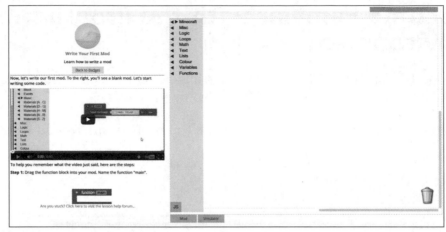

Figure 1-15

Take a look at these four areas of the page:

- *Upper left corner:* Shows the badge name; its large, round icon; and the Back to Badges button, which takes you back to the screen you see in Figure 1-14.

  You can also click the Learn tab at the top of the screen to return to the list of badges.

- *Left column:* Consists of a set of instructions. A short video is always available to explain the badge, followed by a list of steps that spell out what to do.

- *Right side:* Shows the programming environment. In this book you can read how to program using a block-based language that is visual, though you can try a text-based language, *JavaScript,* on your own, too. To access the block-based coding blocks, you click on one of the code categories, such as Minecraft, and click to choose a block to drag into the blank programming area. This process is described in more detail in the next section.

- *Lower center:* Holds two buttons — Mod and Simulator. In this book, you use the Mod button to send your mod to the Minecraft testing world. Clicking the Simulator button opens a Minecraft simulated world in your browser, as shown in Figure 1-16. You use the Minecraft simulator to test your mod to earn the badge.

To enter the simulator, click anywhere in the simulator area. To close the simulator, click the Simulator button again, or press the Esc key on the keyboard.

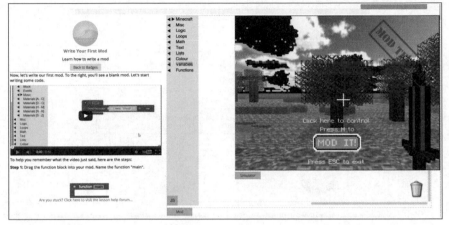

Figure 1-16

After you complete the challenge and test it in the simulator, a badge pops up, as shown in Figure 1-17. You can exit this badge by clicking the Back to Badges button.

Figure 1-17

Write Your First Minecraft Mod

When you're ready to write your first Minecraft mod, click on the Learn tab to go back to the list of badges, and then click on the Write Your First Mod badge, as shown in Figure 1-18.

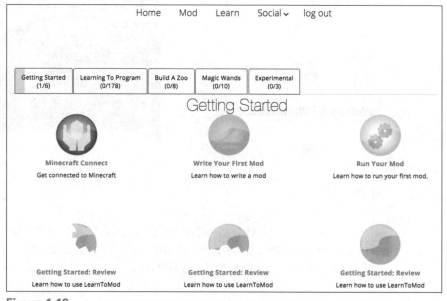

Figure 1-18

In this section, I describe how to earn the second badge. You can also find these steps in the left column of the badge by watching a video or reading written instructions.

You should watch the video before continuing.

You use a function in this challenge. A *function* is a way to group tasks together and name them. For example, if you write a function named `jump rope`, it might contain the tasks `hop` and `spin rope`. I tell you more about functions in Chapter 2.

To earn the second badge, follow these steps:

1. Drag a function into the programming environment and rename it **main**. Figure 1-19 shows where to find the `function` block.

Figure 1-19

2. Click on the text `do something`, as shown in Figure 1-20.

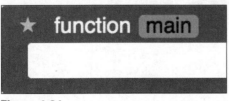

Figure 1-20

3. Type **main** to create a `main` function, as shown in Figure 1-21.

Figure 1-21

4. Click on the Minecraft category and then Players, as shown in Figure 1-22.

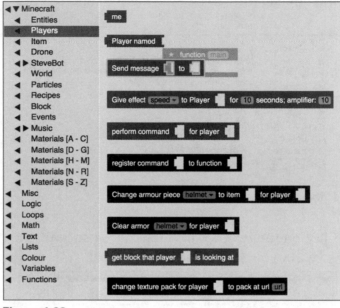

Figure 1-22

5. Click to select the send message block, and then drag it to connect it to the main function, as shown in Figure 1-23.

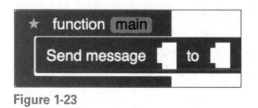

Figure 1-23

6. Click to select the Text code category, as shown in Figure 1-24, and then locate the text block.

7. Drag the text block to connect it to the send message block, and then type **Hello, World!** inside the text block. Figure 1-25 shows how to do this step.

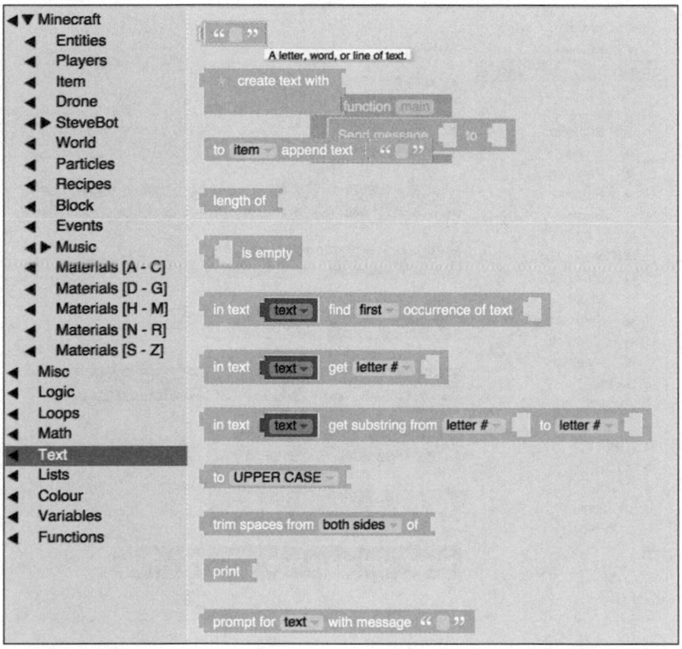

Figure 1-24

Figure 1-25

8. Click the Minecraft category and then Players, as shown in Figure 1-26. Then locate the me block.

9. Drag the me block and connect it to the second space on the send message block, as shown in Figure 1-27.

10. At the bottom of the four steps for this challenge, click the Test In Simulator button, as shown in Figure 1-28.

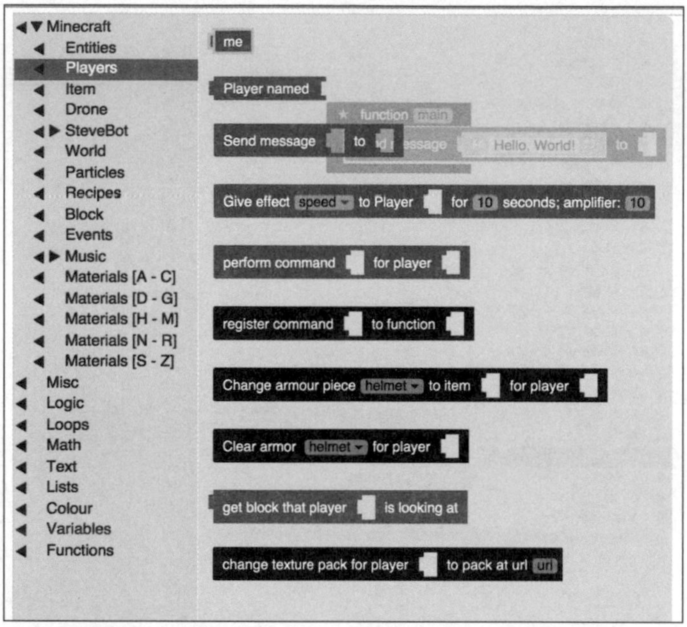

Figure 1-26

Figure 1-27

11. Click in the simulator, and then press the M key on your keyboard. You see the message `Hello, World!` (see Figure 1-29).

12. When the badge you have earned pops up, you can click Back to Badges, as shown in Figure 1-30.

Congratulations! You have written your first Minecraft mod. In the next section, you test your mod in Minecraft.

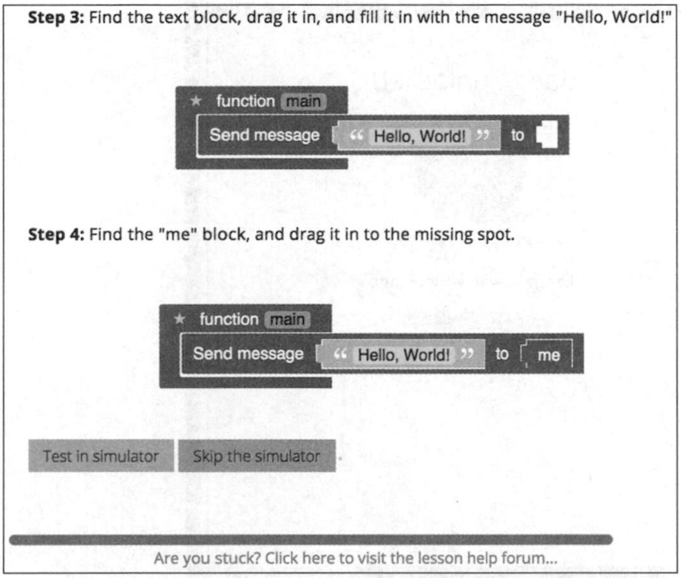
Step 3: Find the text block, drag it in, and fill it in with the message "Hello, World!"
function main
Send message " Hello, World! " to
Step 4: Find the "me" block, and drag it in to the missing spot.
function main
Send message " Hello, World! " to me
Test in simulator
Skip the simulator
Are you stuck? Click here to visit the lesson help forum...

Figure 1-28

Mod loaded! Press M to run it.
Alternative solutions possible. When you run your mod we'll check your answer against the correct one and see if you've discovered an alternative solution.
Hello, World!
Click here to control.
Press M to
MOD IT!
Press ESC to exit.

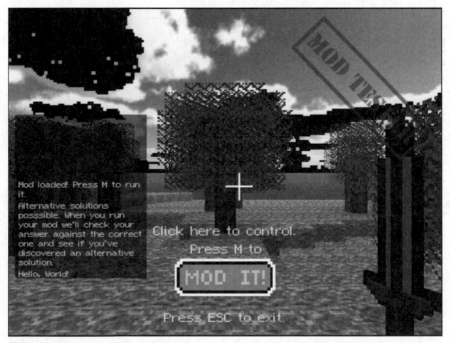

Figure 1-29

Figure 1-30

 You can select the link on the progress bar at the top or ask a question by clicking the link in the upper right corner of the screen, as shown in Figure 1-31.

Figure 1-31

Run Your First Mod in Minecraft

After you write your first mod, the next task you take on is to run the mod in Minecraft. The third badge, Run Your Mod (refer to Figure 1-18), spells out the steps to do this:

1. Click the Mod button at the bottom of the programming environment.

   You can see the button in the lower left corner of Figure 1-32.

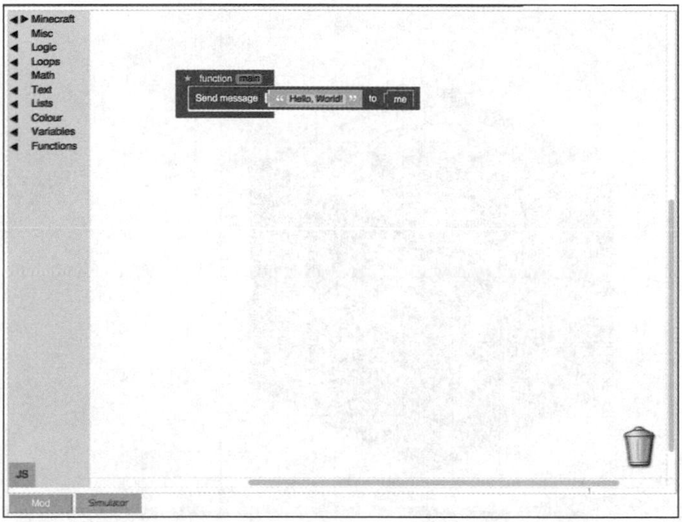

Figure 1-32

When you click on it, you see a message, shown in Figure 1-33, letting you know that the mod was successfully sent to your Minecraft account.

Mod	Simulator

Done! Run your mod with: **/js YourMinecraftUsername.first_mod.main()**

Figure 1-33

2. Click the Minecraft icon on the taskbar of your computer, as shown in Figure 1-34.

You're still in the testing world, so you see the mod chest in the inventory, as shown in Figure 1-35.

REMEMBER

If you aren't already in this world, go back to the Minecraft Connect badge and reconnect, as described in the earlier section "Connect your mods to Minecraft."

Figure 1-34

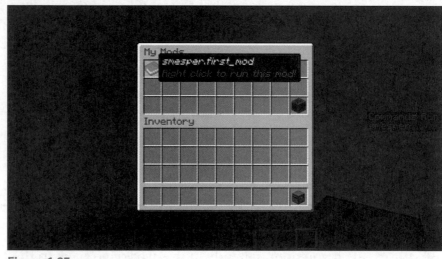

Figure 1-35

3. To equip your mod and use it in Minecraft, follow these steps
while you're in Minecraft:

a. Open the mod chest by pressing 9, and then right-click the
mouse button.

b. Choose the mod that you want to run, and drag it from the mod chest to the inventory. Hover the mouse cursor over different mods to see their names appear.

c. Press the Esc key to exit the mod chest and return to playing.

d. Run your mod by pressing the number that corresponds with the position of the mod in the inventory.

For example, if you place the mod block all the way to the left, as shown in Figure 1-36, you press the 1 key and then right-click the mouse button to run the mod.

Figure 1-36

Return to the LearnToMod website and see that you have earned the third badge. You should then complete the next three challenges, which are quiz badges. I don't walk you through these three badges, because you should be testing your knowledge and earn them on your own.

Write Your Own Minecraft Mods

In Chapter 2, I walk you through the next set of badges on the Learning to Program tab. After you have earned at least ten badges, you might have an idea for your own creative mod that you want to write. Follow these steps:

1. Scroll to the top of the LearnToMod online software and click on the Mod tab, shown in Figure 1-37.

Home	Mod	Learn	Social ⌄	log out

Figure 1-37

2. The new page, shown in Figure 1-38, opens. On this page you can type a title for your mod, such as **Say_Hello**.

Figure 1-38

3. Click the Blockly (Multiplayer) button to create a server-side mod. This book shows you how to make *server-side* mods, which means that they're multiplayer.

A new mod block appears, as shown in Figure 1-39.

Figure 1-39

4. Click on the new mod block to show the mod's description page (see Figure 1-40).

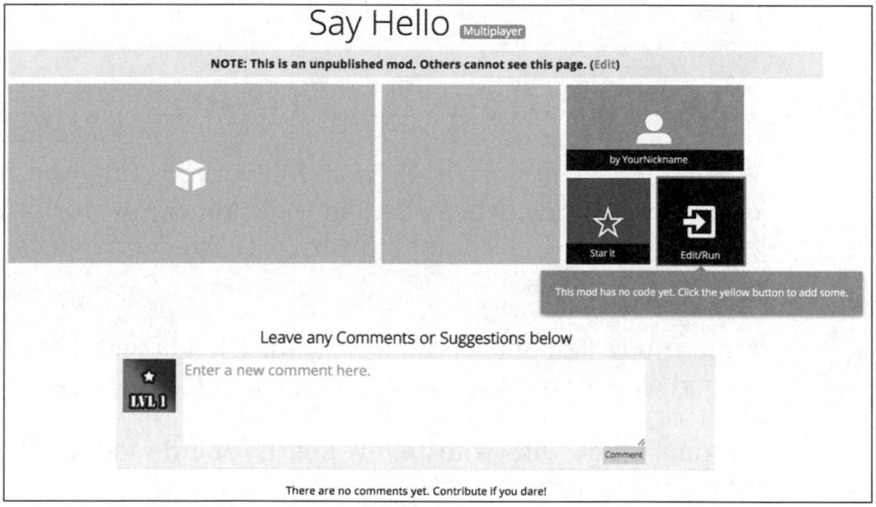

Figure 1-40

5. Click the Code button.

You see the programming environment, as shown in Figure 1-41.

Now you can try writing a new mod — for example, one that says hello to you personally (see Figure 1-42).

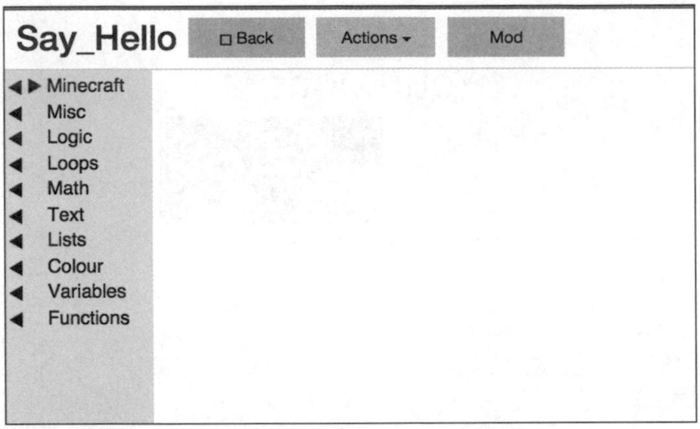

Say_Hello ☐ Back   Actions ▾   Mod

◀ ▶ Minecraft
◀   Misc
◀   Logic
◀   Loops
◀   Math
◀   Text
◀   Lists
◀   Colour
◀   Variables
◀   Functions

Figure 1-41

★ function main
Send message   " Hi Sarah! "   to   me

Figure 1-42

Share Your Mods with Friends

Writing mods and testing them in Minecraft is fun, but being able to have your friends test them in their Minecraft worlds can help you *and* your friends come up with creative mods, because you can get new ideas.

After you write some code, have your friends test it for you — it's a good way to find bugs and become a better modder.

Sharing a mod with your fellow LearnToMod modders is easy. Just follow these steps:

1. Click on the Back button in your mod (refer to Figure 1-41).

2. Click on the image box on the top left, as shown in Figure 1-43.

3. Add a screen shot and description for the mod, by following the steps as shown in Figure 1-44.

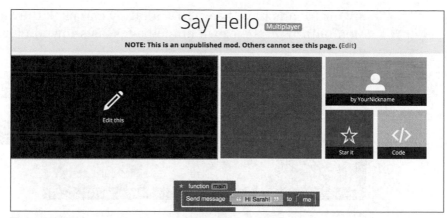

Figure 1-43

Figure 1-44

4. Click the indicator to make the mod public, as shown in Figure 1-45, and then click the Save button.

Figure 1-45

If your friends have LearnToMod, they can click the Find a Mod button on their own home pages, as shown in Figure 1-46.

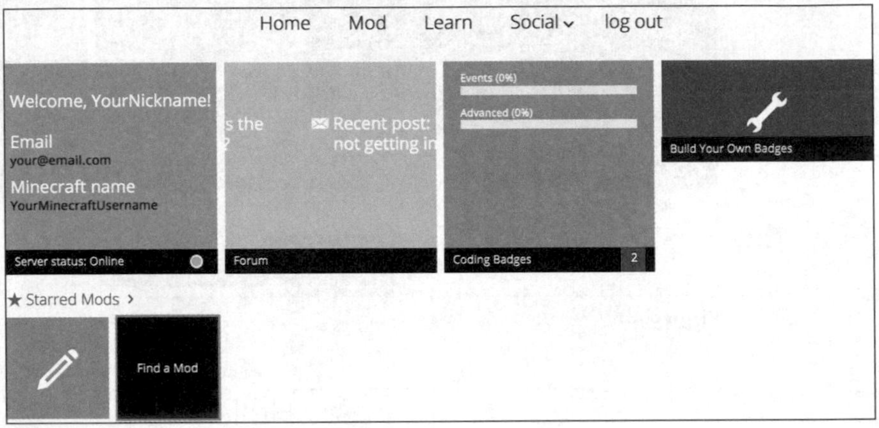

Figure 1-46

Then they can search for your mod, named Say_Hello, as shown in Figure 1-47.

Figure 1-47

Your mod appears, as shown in Figure 1-48. The other person can click on it to test it and see your code.

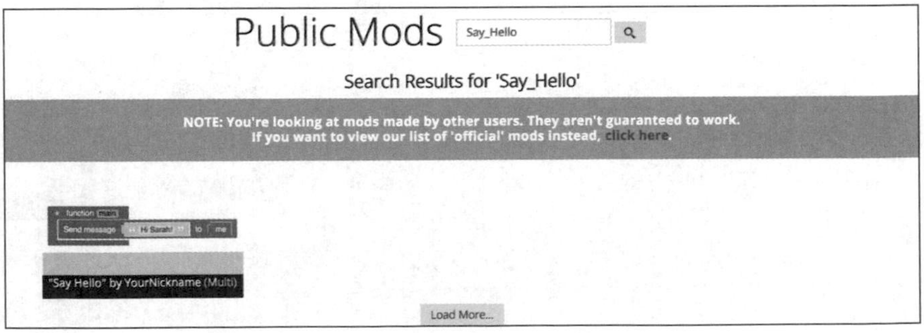

Figure 1-48

Earning Modding Badges

In this project, I help you grasp the basic concepts of programming, by completing challenges and earning badges. I give you the steps to earn different kinds of badges while learning about functions, and I encourage you to try writing your own mods (see the end of Project 1).

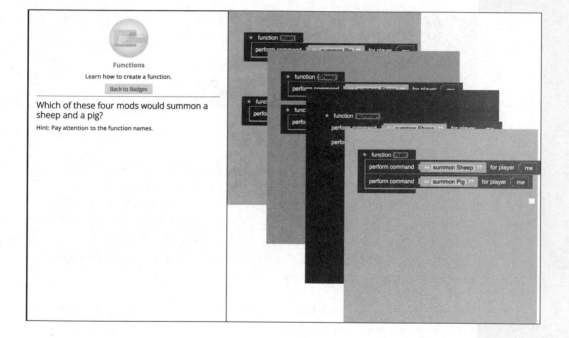

Write Mods with Functions

In Project 1, I describe how to write a mod that has a function named `main` (refer to Figure 1-27, over in Project 1). From now on, I'll call it the `main` function. When you run a mod in Minecraft, your mod always starts running from the `main` function.

Notice that the Saying Hello badge is similar to the Write Your First Mod badge, except that it has three messages instead of two. Figure 2-1 shows the code you should write to complete the Saying Hello badge.

```
★ to main
    Send message  ( " Hello "      to    me
    Send message  ( " How are you? "   to    me
    Send message  ( " My name is Steve. "   to    me
```

Figure 2-1

To get help with completing badges, click the Click for Hints link on the progress bar at the top of the mod, or watch the video to see how to solve the challenge. Sometimes it's tricky to position the blocks in the right spot, so you can always reorder them after you have applied them to your programming environment, though. Later in this book, I introduce you to the cut-and-paste process to make coding even faster.

To earn the badge, you have to test your mod in the Minecraft simulator on the LearnToMod site. The progress bar in this mod says that you have completed writing 100 percent of the code, but it reminds you to test the code in the simulator (see Figure 2-2).

To test your mod in the simulator, click the Simulator button, which is next to the Mod button (see Figure 2-3).

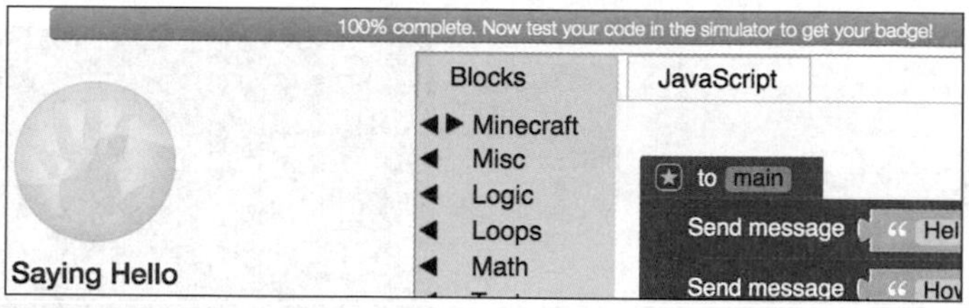

Figure 2-2

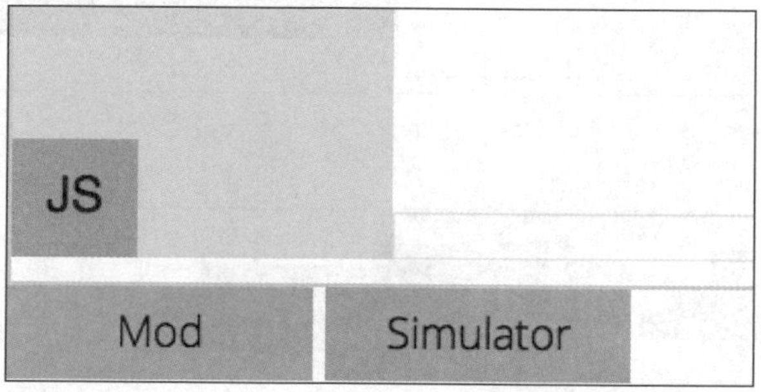

Figure 2-3

The Minecraft simulator sometimes doesn't work in older versions of browsers. If you download the Unity Player plugin and the simulator still doesn't work, update your browser or use a different one. You can download free and reliable browsers such as Chrome, Safari, or Firefox.

Unity Player is the third-party software that supports your being able to see Minecraft in the browser.

When you click the Simulator button, the simulator pops up, as shown in Figure 2-4. To test your mod in the simulator, simply press the M key on the keyboard.

After the mod runs, you earn the badge. You see a screen shot of you completing the badge, as shown in Figure 2-5.

To enter the simulator, drag the mouse into it and click anywhere. To exit the simulator, press the Esc key on the keyboard.

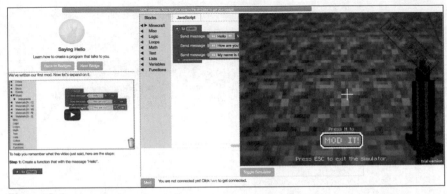

Figure 2-4

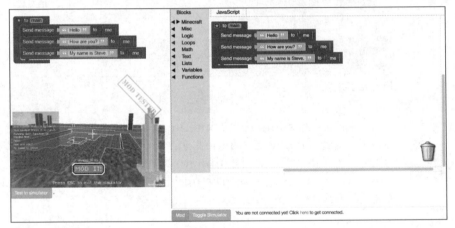

Figure 2-5

Earn Scramble Badges

You can earn a few different kinds of badges. The one I describe earlier in this project is a Code Writing badge. To earn it, you write the code that matches the tutorial. In this section, I introduce you to Scramble badges, which are different from the other types: All the code blocks you need are already in the programming area — they're just scrambled around on the screen in an animation.

To earn a Scramble badge, follow these steps:

1. Test the correct version of the code in the simulator or Minecraft to see what it's supposed to do, like saying "Hello, World!"

2. Gather together all blocks that have been scrambled on the screen, by dragging them near each other (see Figure 2-6).

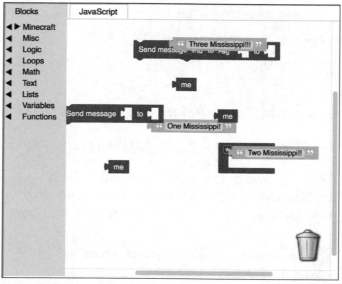

Figure 2-6

3. Unscramble the blocks, and test your mod to see whether it matches the correct version that you test in Step 1 of this list.

To find all the blocks you need in order to complete the badge (sometimes, the blocks that have been scrambled are offscreen), you move around by using the scroll bars on the right side and bottom of the programming environment.

Earn the Saying Hello badge: Scramble Edition

Open the Saying Hello (Scramble) challenge by clicking on the badge, as shown in Figure 2-7.

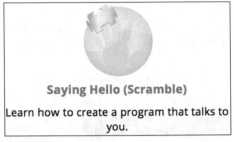

Saying Hello (Scramble)

Learn how to create a program that talks to you.

Figure 2-7

You see ten blocks scrambled on the screen (refer to Figure 2-6).

Follow these steps to solve the challenge and earn the badge:

1. Click the blue Test button to test the correct version in Minecraft, or click the orange Test button to test the correct version in the simulator. Then observe what happens (see Figure 2-8).

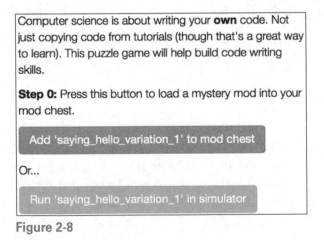

Computer science is about writing your **own** code. Not just copying code from tutorials (though that's a great way to learn). This puzzle game will help build code writing skills.

Step 0: Press this button to load a mystery mod into your mod chest.

Add 'saying_hello_variation_1' to mod chest

Or...

Run 'saying_hello_variation_1' in simulator

Figure 2-8

2. Gather the ten blocks and begin to arrange them in such a way that when you run the mod, it does exactly the same thing that the correct version did.

3. Test your mod in Minecraft or the simulator to see whether it has the same effect as the correct version.

   If it doesn't, edit the blocks arrangement and test again.

4. Continue this edit-test cycle until you have put together the correct arrangement of blocks.

Communicate with your computer

Writing *code* is the way that programmers communicate with their computers, and the way that you communicate with Minecraft. The problem, however, is that computers do exactly what you *tell* them to do, not what you *think* they should do. For example, in the Saying Hello (Scramble) challenge, you may have noticed that the answer looks strange if you expected the messages to be sent in numbered order, like this:

✔ One Mississippi

✔ Two Mississippi

✔ Three Mississippi

and instead they're sent out of order, like this:

✔ Two Mississippi

✔ One Mississippi

✔ Three Mississippi

If you were told, "Go to your shoes and put on your room," you probably would figure out that what you *should* do is go to your *room* and put on your *shoes*. If you told a computer, "Go to your shoes and put on your room," the computer would literally go to its shoes and then try to put on its room, which is impossible, so it would probably display an error message.

You *must* be precise when you write code, and — more importantly — you should test your code often and in small increments to catch mistakes.

At the bottom of any Scramble challenge are two videos (as shown in Figure 2-9) that you can watch to see strategies for completing this type of badge.

Here's a video that will teach you a helpful strategy for these kinds of puzzles:

Here's a video that will show you a terrible strategy:

Figure 2-9

Though the videos aren't specific to each challenge, watching them can help you with any badge that asks you to unscramble code.

Earn Missing Badges

A *Missing* badge has nearly completed code that is missing only a few blocks. Your challenge? To figure out which blocks are missing and where to place them. Without those missing blocks, the mod cannot run.

As with a Scramble badge, you use a smart strategy to earn a Missing badge. Follow these steps:

1. Identify how many blocks are missing, and identify where they're missing. Start thinking about what type of blocks might be missing, such as a `text` block.

2. Test the correct version of the code in the simulator (by clicking the blue Test button) or Minecraft (by clicking the orange Test button) to see what it's supposed to do.

3. Follow the code as it's running, and identify where the missing blocks should be placed. (Read the following section for tips on following code.)

4. Add in the blocks that are missing, and test your code to see whether it accomplishes the same result as the correct version does in Step 1 of this list. This is what professional coders do: They follow their code while they're testing it, to ensure that they have told the computer to do the right thing.

Trace code

Coders make mistakes, and communicating with computers can be tricky.

Coders (like you) should be sure to follow the code, before and while it's running, to ensure that you put the lines of code in the correct order.

Tracing code is an important skill to master, and you can do it in multiple ways. Here are two helpful code tracing strategies:

- **Use the computer.** Especially for Missing badges, this is a great way to trace code. First, run your code (or the correct version) and watch what happens. Then run the code again, but this time point to each line of code as it's being run. For example, when you see the `Hello, World!` message, point to the line of code shown in Figure 2-10. Then you can figure out what is happening in the correct code when your code has a missing block.

- **Use pencil and paper.** If you have a written mod that isn't working the way you expect, draw on paper what is happening after each line of code executes. For example, the code shown in Figure 2-10, `Send Message "Hello, World!" to me` will be printed to the screen, so you should write it down on paper.

Figure 2-10

Earn the Saying Hello badge: Missing Edition

Open the Saying Hello (Missing) challenge by clicking on the badge. When you earn the badge, the code makes part of the lyrics to a Cat Stevens song print to the screen (see Figure 2-11).

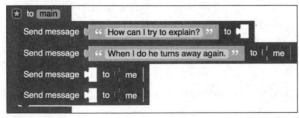

Figure 2-11

Three blocks are missing from this mod. The first is probably a `player` block because that's the only player you have used and that's what the other ones are using. The last two are likely to be `text` blocks because that's the only kind of message you have sent, and the first two are sending text messages too. It's impossible to guess what text should be placed in the `text` blocks, because the list of possibilities is *very, very large*.

To complete a missing badge, follow these steps:

1. Run the correct version in Minecraft or the simulator and watch what happens. When you run your code, you should see the scene shown in Figure 2-12.

Figure 2-12

The first line of code sends the message How can I try to explain? but doesn't specify which player is the target of the message (the one that will receive the message). After running the code, you can see that the target should be the me block because *you* can see that message when *you* run the correct version (see Figure 2-13) and the last two messages are

```
It has always been the same,
same old story . . .
```

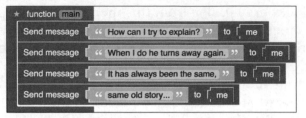

Figure 2-13

Everything sent to me shows up on the screen of the person who ran the mod. So, if you run the mod and you see the message, the target of the message was me.

2. Add in the me block and the two text blocks with the correct messages in them (refer to Figure 2-13). Then test your mod, to be sure that it does the same thing as the correct version does (refer to Figure 2-12).

If you return to a Missing badge or Scramble badge after completing it, the LearnToMod software asks whether you want to reset the code so that it's missing or scrambled again. If you choose to reset your badge, you will still have the badge. You just get to attempt the challenge again.

Make and Call New Functions

A function is a way to group a lot of code and then name it. You *make* a new function (or *define* or *write* a new function) when you drag a function block, change its name, and add code inside it. You *call* a function when you drag the specific function block into another function, like the main function.

Here are the primary characteristics of the main function:

✔ Each mod has exactly one main function. Your mod starts at the main function, so you need to have at least one. If you had two or more, your mod wouldn't know which one to start with. In fact, to avoid this type of confusion, each function must have a name that's different from any other function in that mod.

✔ You can create the main function by dragging a function block into the programming environment and naming it main.

✔ The other coding blocks, like send message, are inside the main function.

✔ Minecraft and the simulator first look for the main function and then begin running the code inside it, from top to bottom, line by line.

The main function is essential for writing mods, but there are reasons for having other functions, too. In the same way that chapters in a book let you group ideas and name those ideas, functions allow you to group code and name the grouping that results.

Figure 2-14 shows an example of a long main function. In this mod, two stories are being told: The Three Pigs and Goldilocks and The Three Bears.

Figure 2-14

On Line 13 of the code, you can see that the modder misspelled *accidentally* as *axidentaly* (see Figure 2-15). Someone might catch this mistake while testing the mod, but finding it will be difficult because you have to read each word.

Figure 2-15

Finding the problem is much easier if the code uses other functions, as shown in Figure 2-16, because then you can look for the error only in the `Goldilocks and The Three Bears` function.

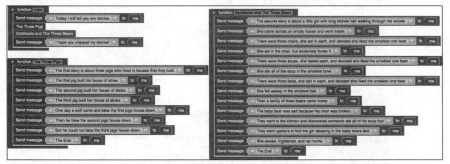

Figure 2-16

Having shorter functions is useful because then you can rearrange large parts of the code quickly. Figure 2-17 shows how simply swapping two lines of code can change the order in which the stories are told.

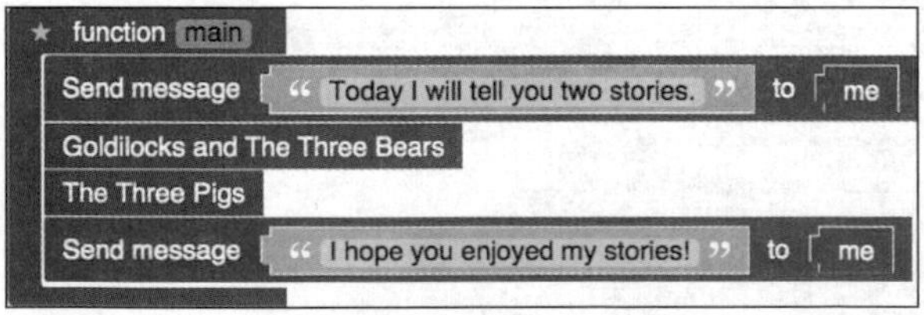

Figure 2-17

Complete the Functions Badge Code

In the following sections, I walk you through completing the Functions challenge and earning the Functions badge. To start, be sure that you have opened the Functions challenge by clicking on the badge.

By the time you reach the end of this section, you will know how to define two new functions: `creeper1` and `creeper2`. The final code that you write is shown in Figure 2-18. When you test this code, you see the scene shown in Figure 2-19.

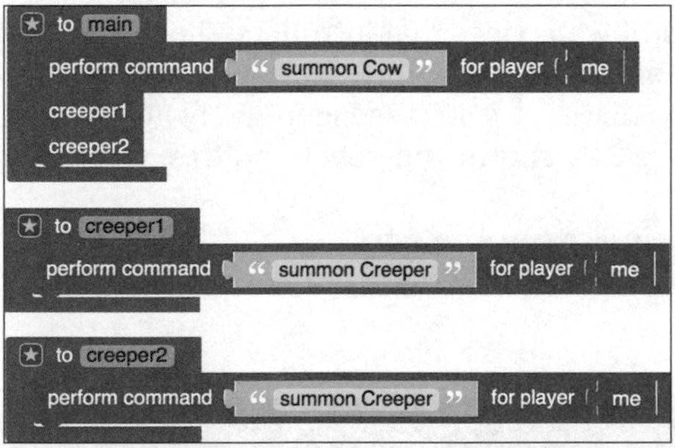

Figure 2-18

Figure 2-19

Use the Perform Command block

In the Functions badge, the block named `perform command` performs the command that is in the `text` block for a certain player, as defined by the `player` block. Figure 2-20 shows the `perform command` block, which summons a cow to you.

Figure 2-20

Minecraft has a set of commands that you can run from inside the game. You can search the Internet for the term *Minecraft commands* to see millions of web pages that introduce them. For example, if you want to summon a cow without writing a mod, you can type the command /`summon Cow` (see Figure 2-21) in Minecraft to summon one. Figure 2-22 shows you how to do this.

Figure 2-21

Figure 2-22

To make Minecraft run the `perform command` block, you have to place the block inside the `main` function, as shown in Figure 2-23.

```
★ to main
perform command ❝ summon Cow ❞ for player me
```

Figure 2-23

Test your code at this point, to make sure that it does what you want. When you run this code in Minecraft, you see a scene similar to the one shown in Figure 2-24.

Figure 2-24

Create and call a new function

As you can see in the completed code for this challenge (refer to Figure 2-18), you need to define two new functions. Define the first one and test your code to make sure it works. Then define the second one. If you finish writing your code without testing it, you make errors harder to find, because you'll have lots of code to trace.

To create and then call the `creeper` function, follow these steps:

1. Drag a `function` block into the programming environment.

2. Click on the words `do something` and rename the function **creeper,** as shown in Figure-25.

Figure 2-25

3. Add a `perform command` block in the `creeper` function and type **summon creeper** in the text area, as shown in Figure 2-26.

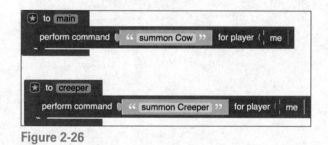

Figure 2-26

4. Run your mod in Minecraft or the simulator.

   Notice that only a cow is summoned, not a creeper. The reason is that only the `main` function is called (from Minecraft or the simulator). You did not *call* the `creeper` function, so it's ignored.

5. When you view the Functions category, notice that a new block has been created — the `creeper` call block, shown in Figure 2-27.

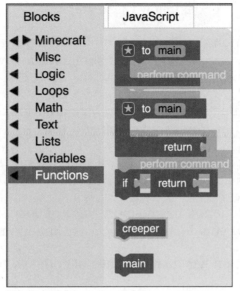

Figure 2-27

6. Call `creeper` from the `main` function, as shown in Figure 2-28.

Figure 2-28

7. Run your mod in Minecraft or the simulator.

A cow and a creeper are summoned.

Trace function calls

To better understand what is happening when you run your mod, trace your code using the paper-and-pencil strategy described in the section "Trace code," earlier in this project.

To trace each line of code, follow these steps:

1. The `main` function is called, and the first thing it does is run the `perform command` block that summons a cow, and that makes a cow appear, so draw a cow.

2. The `creeper` function is called, so Minecraft looks into the `creeper` function. You should look at it too.

3. When the `perform command` block that summons a creeper is run, it makes a creeper appear, so draw a creeper.

   The `creeper` function has no more lines of code, Minecraft looks back (and you do, too) to the `main` function.

   The `main` function has no more lines of code, so the code is complete.

Add a second Creeper function

In the same way you created the first `creeper` function, create the second `creeper` function. Step 3 in the Functions challenge gives you instructions on this task, as shown in Figure 2-29.

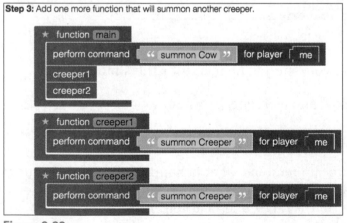

Figure 2-29

If you need help, you can ask questions in the Comment area below the badge by clicking the Are You Stuck? link, shown in Figure 2-30.

Figure 2-30

Earn Quiz Badges

As you use the LearnToMod software, you run into opportunities to earn Quiz badges, such as the Functions Quiz badge, shown in Figure 2-31. Earning a Quiz badge can be tricky, so be sure to read the entire question and all answer choices carefully.

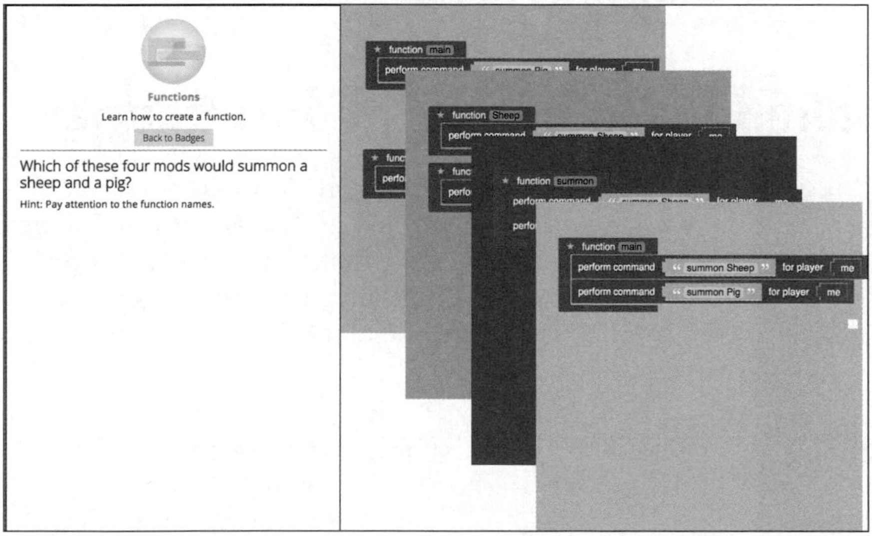

Figure 2-31

If it helps, use a pencil and paper to work through the quiz question, especially when you begin using drones in Project 3.

When you think you have the correct answer, just click on the colored box that holds the answer choice. If you answer incorrectly, you see the message shown in Figure 2-32. Otherwise, you earn the badge, and you can move on.

Figure 2-32

Challenge Yourself Beyond Badges

Earning badges can be a lot of fun, but I want you to be able to create your own mods, not just follow along with badges. In this section, you face a challenge that has no badge associated with it. If you get stuck at any point, just ask questions in the LearnToMod forum by clicking on the Social tab from the home page, as shown in Figure 2-33.

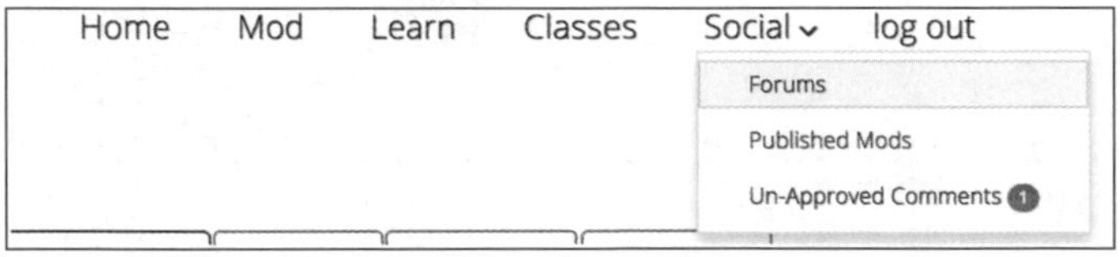

Figure 2-33

Complete the Function Challenge

Before you attempt the challenge in this section, you should have earned at least five badges from the Functions challenges.

To write a mod from scratch (see the section in Project 1 about writing your own Minecraft mods), go to your home page and click the Mod link at the top of the page, as shown in Figure 2-34.

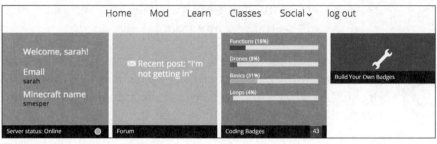

Figure 2-34

Name your mod `function_challenge_1` and choose Blockly (Multiplayer) as the language. Click on the mod block and then the Code button until you get to the programming environment. It should look like Figure 2-35.

Figure 2-35

Write a mod that has these four functions:

- ✔ summonCreepers function: Summons two creepers

- ✔ summonZombies function: Summons three zombies

- ✔ summonCreatures function: Summons four creepers and three zombies by calling the summonCreepers and summon-Zombies functions

- ✔ main function: Summons two sets of creatures by calling the summonCreatures function.

As an extra challenge before you run the completed code, predict how many total zombies and creepers will be summoned. Predicting what your code will do is a useful way to help you determine whether you've written the code correctly.

The final code should have only 14 lines of code. If you need help, see the solution code in Figure 2-36. (But try not to peek ahead of time!)

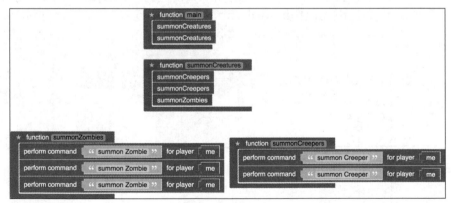

Figure 2-36

A block of code is different from a line of code. One block of code can be the me block, whereas one line of code can be three blocks of code, like the `perform command` block with a `text` block and a me block. When you're counting lines of code, the completed `perform command` is considered one line. When you're counting blocks of code, the completed `perform command` is considered three blocks. An empty function is considered one block and one line of code.

Building and Protecting Structures

In this project, I walk you through the steps to build and protect structures in your Minecraft world. First I describe how to build small structures like towers, and then I progress into how to build complex, intricate structures like houses, castles, and villages. I tell you how to build a structure brick by brick, how to protect your structures with lightning, and then how to use loops to build them faster.

Use Drones to Build Structures in Minecraft

Building structures is made much easier when you can use drones. A *drone* is an invisible robot that can move around and place blocks and entities at its location. In this section, you start building structures in Minecraft using drones — knowledge that comes in handy when you need to build large structures.

For example, in Project 4, I show you how to make the game of Spleef, which requires you to create a platform with a short fence around it and then put lava all over the platform. Then you have to create another platform with a tall fence around it, directly above the first platform you made. Because the platform has to be at least 20 blocks wide, placing the platform brick by brick would take a long time. (That's more than 1,000 blocks!) Instead, you can write a mod that builds these platforms, and you can play lots of versions of the game without having to rebuild it every time.

Create a drone

Creating a drone isn't complicated, but it does require you to use a new coding feature: variables. A *variable* is a way to name an object. In this section, you can follow along with my description of the Drones challenge in the LearnToMod online software.

Open the Drones challenge, and follow these steps:

1. To be able to give commands to the drone, you need to name it. You name an object, like a drone, by assigning it to a variable. First drag a `variable` block into the `main` function, as shown in Figure 3-1.

2. Always give objects names that make sense to you and that you can easily remember. In this example, create a new variable by clicking on the arrow next to `item` (see Figure 3-2) and name it `d`, for *d*rone (see Figure 3-3).

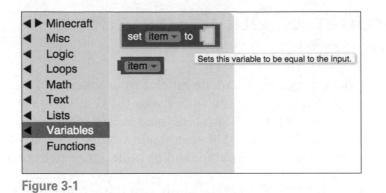

Figure 3-1

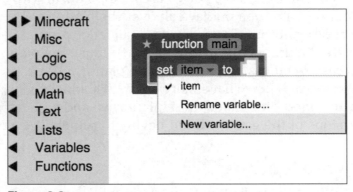

Figure 3-2

Figure 3-3

3. To create a drone, you have to assign a new one to the variable you just made. Figure 3-4 shows where you can find the `new Drone` block, and Figure 3-5 shows you where to put it in the `d assign` block.

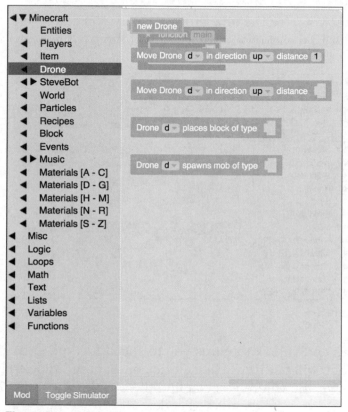

Figure 3-4

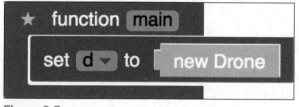

Figure 3-5

Now that you have a drone, you can access it by using its name, d, and you can tell it to perform certain actions, such as place blocks or spawn entities.

Build a structure and move a drone

After you give the new drone a name, you can give it commands. Figure 3-6 shows you where to find the `place block` code block.

◀ ▼ Minecraft
◀　Entities
◀　Players
◀　Item
◀　Drone
◀ ▶ SteveBot
◀　World
◀　Particles
◀　Recipes
◀　Block
◀　Events
◀ ▶ Music
◀　Materials [A - C]
◀　Materials [D - G]
◀　Materials [H - M]
◀　Materials [N - R]
◀　Materials [S - Z]

new Drone
× function main
Move Drone d in direction up distance 1
Move Drone d in direction up distance
Drone d places block of type
Drone d spawns mob of type

Figure 3-6

This code block requires you to specify a type of block that the drone will put down, like a brick or diamond block. Figure 3-7 shows you where you can find the `brick` type, and Figure 3-8 shows you the completed code.

If you run this code in Minecraft or the simulator, you see a scene like the one shown in Figure 3-9.

 Your structure appears in the area in which you're looking, so move to an empty area when you build. I even like to go into Creative mode and build in the sky: Double-click the spacebar to hover, and then press the spacebar again to move upward.

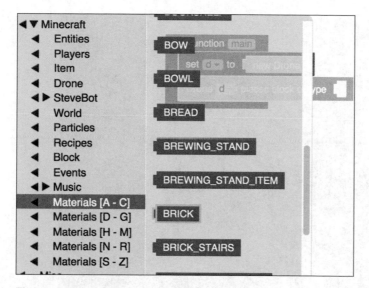

Figure 3-7

Figure 3-8

Continuing with Step 3 of the Drones challenge, you should add a move block to your mod. Figure 3-10 shows the move block that you add. You can find the block under the Minecraft category and then Drones, just like the place block code block you found (refer to Figure 3-6).

If you run the code again, you see the same result shown in Figure 3-9. The drone is invisible, so moving it around has no visible effect.

Continue working to complete this challenge by adding three more lines of code. Figure 3-11 shows the completed code needed to earn this badge.

Figure 3-9

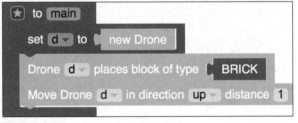

Figure 3-10

Before you run the mod, predict on paper what you will see. Then run the mod in the simulator, and compare your prediction to what you see.

If your prediction was incorrect, go back to the code and trace it either on paper or on the computer. (Visit the "Trace code" section in Project 2 for tips on how to do this.) To trace using the computer, disable all blocks of code by right-clicking and choosing Disable Block (see Figure 3-12). Then reenable one block at a time, testing the mod every time you enable one, to see whether you understand what is going on.

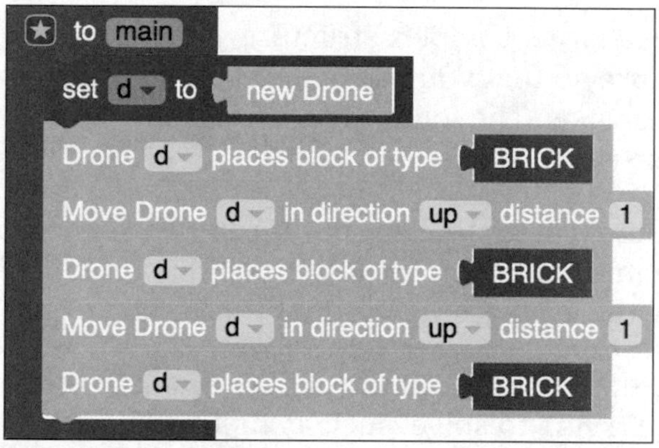

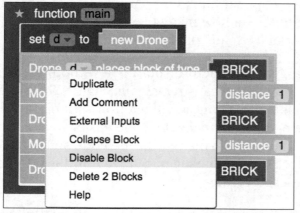

Figure 3-11

Figure 3-12

Build a Tower in Minecraft By Breaking Coding into Phases

Knowing how to create drones, move them, and use them to place blocks allows you to build anything you can imagine. Building large, complex structures, however, requires lots of code, and the whole process can get confusing.

Before making a large, complex structure, explore how to make a smaller structure so that you can understand the mechanics of building with drones. The following sections spell out how to create a tower using drones.

Coding is a complicated process, but it can be broken up into three main segments: design, develop, test. Expert coders cycle through these three stages throughout the coding experience:

✔ **Design:** In this phase, you (the coder) evaluate the problem that you're trying to solve, such as building a tower in Minecraft. You research different ways of solving the problem and come up with a plan of action. Sometimes, this phase requires using paper and pencil. You draw a tower on paper and make notes on how many blocks high the tower is, and what material it's made of, like brick.

Sometimes, you restructure your code without changing what it does — that's known as *refactoring*. Figure 2-14 (over in Project 2) is quite a long `main` function with multiple stories being told. To make the code easier to see without changing the stories, you *refactor* the code so that it looks like Figure 2-16. The code changes, but what it does (tell two stories) doesn't change.

✔ **Develop:** In this phase, you write the code that follows the plan of action from the design phase. Sometimes you hit a roadblock (you didn't think about how wide the tower should be, for example) and you have to return to the design phase to redesign some or all of the solution.

✔ **Test:** In this phase, you test the code you wrote to make sure that it does what you want in all cases. Testing can be *complicated,* so coders write test cases.

For example, if your program is supposed to add two numbers, test to make sure that all the following test cases pass (examples are included):

- Two positive numbers should make a positive number: 2+5 = 7.

- Two negative numbers should make a negative number: $-5 + -3 = -8$.

- A positive number and a negative number results in subtracting the negative number from the positive number: $-9 + 5 = -4$.

- A letter and a number should return an error.

- Two letters should return an error: a + b = ERROR.

- Large numbers should add together: 500 + 289 = 789.

- A mixture of numbers, letters, or any other symbols (@, for example) should return an error: hf7w + 9 = ERROR.

Consider all the ways the code should work, and all the ways it shouldn't. You may find a test case that doesn't work, so you'll have to return to the development or design phase. Finding and fixing bugs is one of the most time-consuming areas of coding, but if you find the bugs in early cycles, coding becomes much faster.

Sometimes the code you write is simple, so cycling through these three phases isn't complicated. But as you start writing larger and more complex code, it becomes more important to make sure you're completing all three phases. If you go straight to coding and don't design or test, you will definitely have bugs in your code and your program won't work how you expect it to.

Design: Sketch out the tower

You can design code to build a tower in many different ways. In this section, I show you how to design it by drawing it on paper or using real-life blocks to build it:

1. Sketch or build the tower as it would appear in Minecraft. If you're drawing it on paper, this step can be difficult because paper is 2-dimensional (2D) and Minecraft is 3-dimensional (3D). The drawing doesn't have to be perfect, however — you just need to form an idea of what it takes to make a tower (such as how many blocks or what type of block). Figure 3-13 shows two sides of a tower.

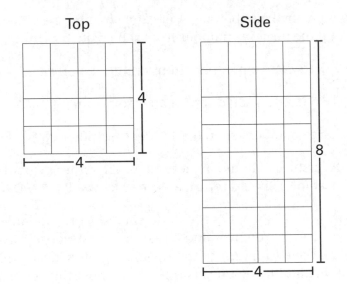

Figure 3-13

2. On a piece of paper, break your design into manageable pieces.

Figure 3-14 shows one way to do it:

- *One row of blocks:* Indicates where the drone is moving.

- *Two rows of blocks:* Show how you need to reset the drone for each row. That means the drone will have to move back to the beginning of the row, before moving up.

- *One full square of blocks:* Indicates an entire square, which requires 16 blocks. The tower consists of 8 squares arranged on top of each other.

- *Two rows of squares:* Show how you need to reset the drone for each column.

- *Four rows of squares:* Ensure that you're still on the right track.

- *Eight rows of squares:* The Tower.

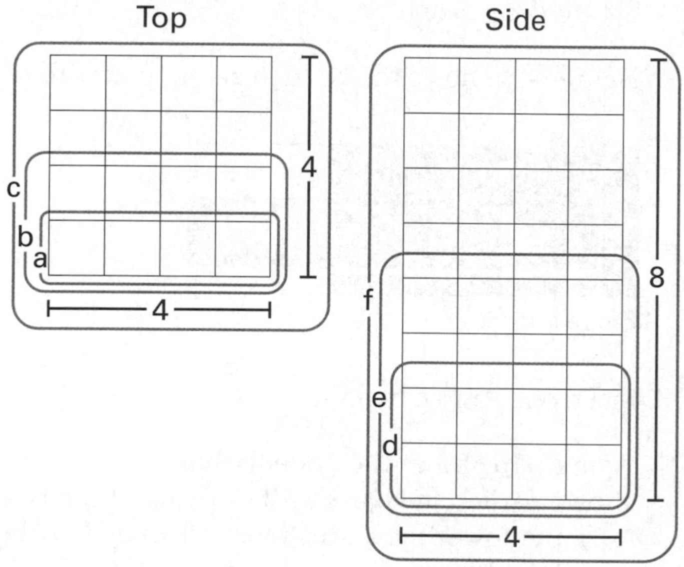

Figure 3-14

Development and testing: Write code for the tower

During the development phase, you build each of the six chunks of your tower from the previous section (refer to Figure 3-14). When you write the code for each chunk, test it to make sure that it does what you want.

Create a new mod named Tower using Blockly as the language.

(Project 1 describes how to make a new mod that isn't a badge. Revisit the section "Writing Your Own Minecraft Mods" if you can't remember how to make a new one.)

Before you begin this step list, read the earlier section "Use Drones to Build Structures in Minecraft" and make sure you have earned the first Drones badge. To build and test the tower, follow these steps:

1. Set up your drone.

   Figure 3-15 shows the code to set up your drone to build a tower.

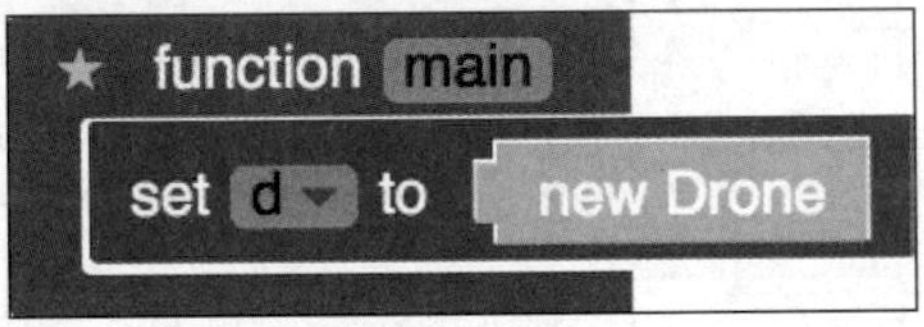

   ★ function main

   set d to   new Drone

   Figure 3-15

2. Make one row of blocks.

   Figure 3-16 shows the code to make one row of blocks. As shown earlier, in Figure 3-13 (looking at the tower from the top), the tower measures four bricks by four bricks, so each row should have four bricks in it.

3. Test the code to ensure that it makes one row of blocks.

   Figure 3-17 shows what the row of blocks should look like.

The structure will appear in the area in which you're looking, so it's best to go to an empty area when you build. I even like to go into Creative mode and build in the sky: Double-click the spacebar to hover, and then press the spacebar to move upward.

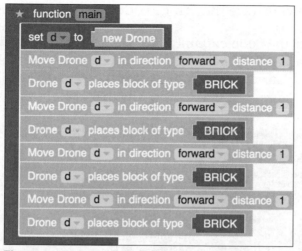

Figure 3-16

Figure 3-17

4. Make two rows of blocks by copying the first row.

Figure 3-18 shows the code for making two rows.

5. Trace the code (see the "Trace code" section in Project 2).

Look over the code carefully, and sketch out what you think the drone will do. Figure 3-19 shows one way to sketch it out and trace your code. And, in case you're wondering, it doesn't make two rows — it makes one row that is eight blocks long.

```
★ function main
set d to    new Drone
Move Drone d in direction forward distance 1
Drone d places block of type   BRICK
Move Drone d in direction forward distance 1
Drone d places block of type   BRICK
Move Drone d in direction forward distance 1
Drone d places block of type   BRICK
Move Drone d in direction forward distance 1
Drone d places block of type   BRICK
Move Drone d in direction forward distance 1
Drone d places block of type   BRICK
Move Drone d in direction forward distance 1
Drone d places block of type   BRICK
Move Drone d in direction forward distance 1
Drone d places block of type   BRICK
Move Drone d in direction forward distance 1
Drone d places block of type   BRICK
```

Figure 3-18

6. Test the code.

You can see that the tracing shown in Figure 3-19 matches what is made in the scene in Figure 3-20.

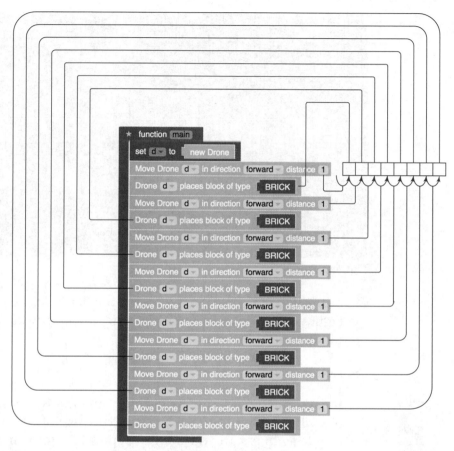

Figure 3-19

7. Edit the code.

Before you add the code to make the second row, reset the drone by moving it back to the right. Then move the drone forward, as shown in Figure 3-21.

Forward and backward are relative to you, the player, not to the drone. So whatever direction you're facing is forward, and the opposite direction is backward.

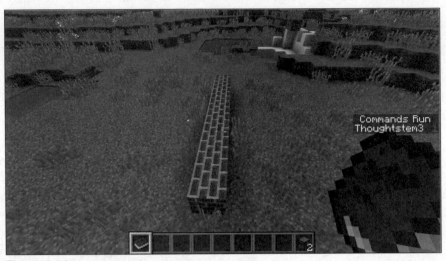

Figure 3-20

8. Test the code again. Doing so produces the scene shown in Figure 3-22: two rows of blocks where each row is four blocks long.

9. Refactor your code.

Refactoring your code means changing the way it looks, but not what it does. This concept is truly useful when your code is getting long and you want to separate it into smaller functions.

The code shown in Figure 3-21 is already starting to get long, and you've made only two rows of blocks. The easiest way to refactor this code is to find the bits that repeat, such as making one row of four blocks, and put them in a separate function. Figure 3-23 shows the same code, refactored to be shorter.

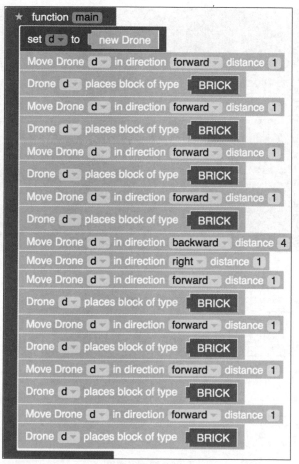

Figure 3-21

10. Make one square of blocks.

   After you have refactored your code, making a 4 x 4 square of blocks should seem simple. Figure 3-24 shows the code to create the structure, and Figure 3-25 shows the result of using that code in Minecraft.

11. Refactor the code again. In Step 9, you refactor the code to make it easier to make multiple rows of four blocks. Now refactor the code to make it easier for you to make multiple rows of 4 x 4 squares. Refactor the code to match Figure 3-26.

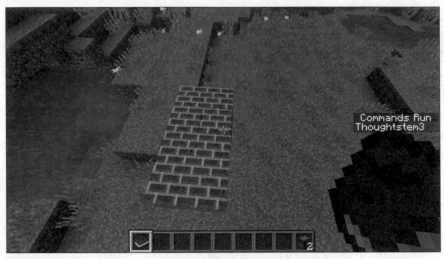

Figure 3-22

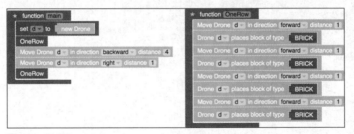

Figure 3-23

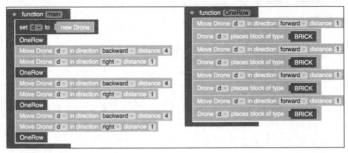

Figure 3-24

Figure 3-25

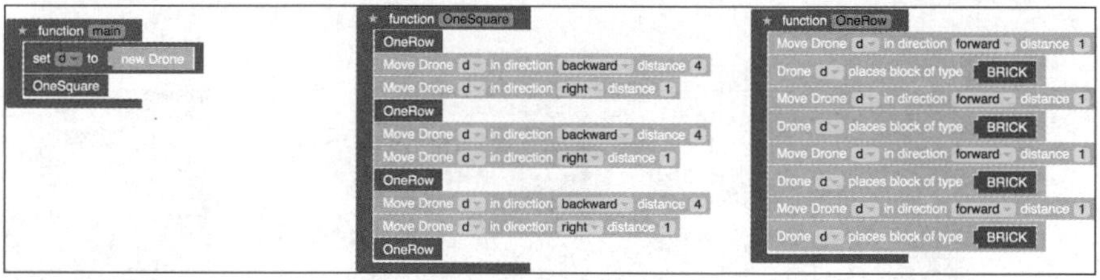

Figure 3-26

12. Make two rows of 4 x 4 squares.

After you can make one square, of course, you can easily make a second square on top of it. The tricky part is to reset the drone correctly. As I show you in Steps 6, 7, and 8, you might need to "test-edit-test" a few times to get it just right. Figures 3-27 and 3-28 show two correct answers for starting to make an actual tower.

13. Make four rows of squares.

Figure 3-29 shows how to make a 4 x 4 tower, starting with the code in Figure 3-28.

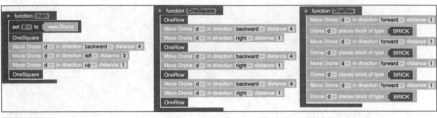

Figure 3-27

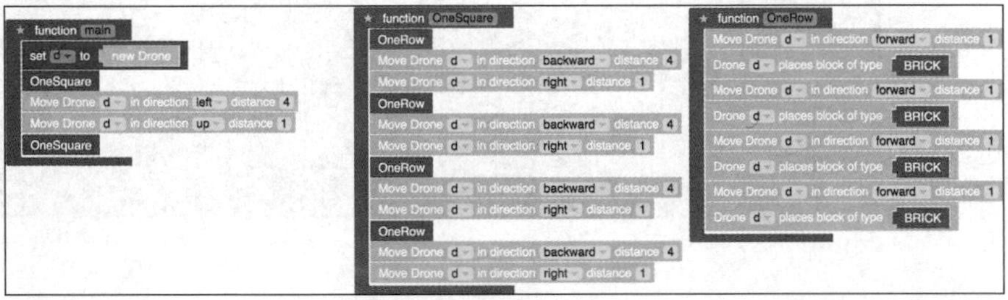

Figure 3-28

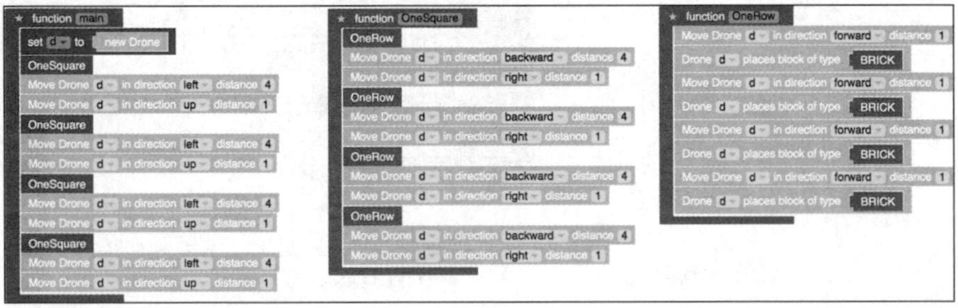

Figure 3-29

14. Make eight rows of squares.

At last, you can make an 8 x 4 tower. Figure 3-30 shows a final refactored version of the tower code.

In the following sections, I show you how to strike lightning in Minecraft, and then you can defend your tower with lightning, by having it strike on all four sides.

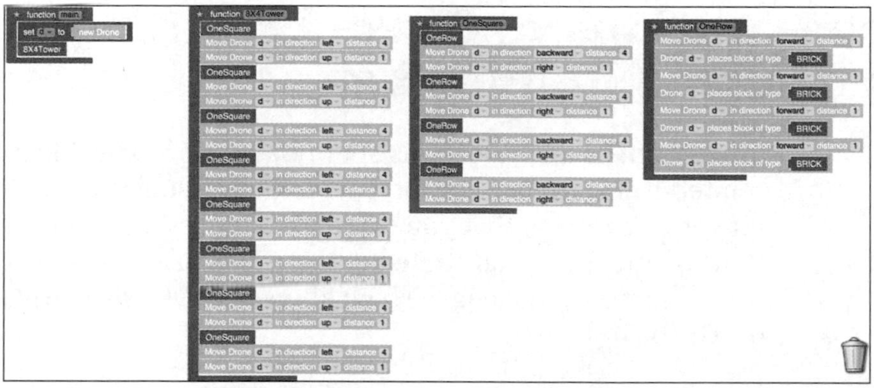

Figure 3-30

Build other tower variations

Whenever you write code, test your understanding by changing the code slightly to do something a little different from normal. This helps you gain an understanding of how the functions are working together, and how to be creative and build other structures as well.

For example, here are a few variations on towers that you can build on your own:

⮞ Build a 3 x 8 tower.

⮞ Build a tower that is in the shape of a triangle instead of a square.

⮞ Build a tower that has fallen over (a horizontal tower).

⮞ Build two towers next to each other.

⮞ Build a walkway between two towers that are next to each other.

   Hint: Build a combination of the fourth and fifth items in this list.

Use Locations to Strike Lightning on Yourself in Minecraft

In the Drones and Locations set of badges are specific badges related to locations. The fun part about having the location of a player or drone is that you can make things happen directly at that location, such as strike lightning. This section describes the first Locations challenge, which shows you how to strike lightning on yourself.

Note: From now on, I'm not walking you through the process of clicking on badges or creating new mods. If you can't remember how to do this, revisit Project 1.

Make sure you're in Creative mode while in Minecraft when you test this badge.

Figure 3-31 shows the final batch of code you write to make lightning strike on yourself.

Figure 3-31

This code example uses two new blocks:

✔ world strike lightning at: You can find it under the Minecraft category and then World, as shown in Figure 3-32.

✔ location of: You can find it under the Minecraft category and then Entities, as shown in Figure 3-33.

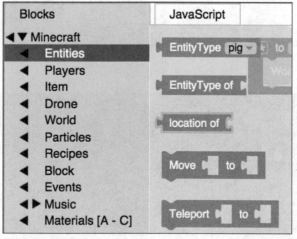

Figure 3-32

Figure 3-33

When you run this mod in either Minecraft or the simulator, two things happen:

- ✔ You see the lightning descend from the sky, as shown in Figure 3-34.

- ✔ The grass around you catches fire (see Figure 3-35).

Figure 3-34

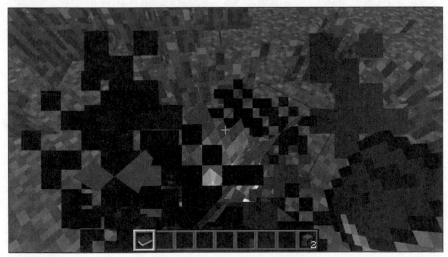

Figure 3-35

Use Locations to Strike Lightning on Drones in Minecraft

In the Locations Part 2 challenge, you can read how to strike lightning on drones rather than on yourself. This information can come in handy when you're trying to defend structures you've created, like the tower I tell you how to make in the earlier section "Building a Tower in Minecraft."

Figure 3-36 shows the code you need in order to strike lightning somewhere other than on yourself.

```
★ function main
    set d to    new Drone
    World strike lightning at    location of    d
```

Figure 3-36

You can strike lightning in multiple places by using multiple drones — neat-o!

Figure 3-37 shows you how to make three drones and strike lightning on each of them.

```
★ function main
    set d to    new Drone
    set c to    new Drone
    set b to    new Drone
    Move Drone c in direction right distance 3
    Move Drone b in direction right distance 6
    World strike lightning at    location of    d
    World strike lightning at    location of    c
    World strike lightning at    location of    b
```

Figure 3-37

Being able to make multiple drones can also come in handy if you want to make multiple structures. Each drone can be in charge of making a different structure, and you don't have to reset one before making something new.

Debug Complex Mods

When the code in your mod isn't working the way you want, such as when you make a row of eight bricks instead of two rows of four bricks, it may have an error, or *bug*. If your code has a bug in it, you have to *debug* it, or fix it. Writing large, complex mods makes it even more likely that you'll run into mistakes that are hard to find.

In this section, I give you four strategies for debugging your code:

✔ **Walk away.** When your code stops making sense, just walk away and watch a video or TV show, and then get back to the task at hand. Sometimes, when you work on one problem for a long time, you miss the error that would be easy to find if you were to simply take a break. Tech companies such as Microsoft, Google, and Facebook often have game rooms with Xbox, PlayStation, foosball, and ping-pong set up so that their programmers can take breaks when they run into tricky bugs.

✔ **Draw using pencil and paper.** The great thing about programming something you can see is that you can trace your code and draw it out on paper. Go line by line and move your pencil just like the drone, and draw a block whenever the drone places a block. That will help you see anything that is going wrong.

✔ **Disable blocks.** In this helpful technique, you add the blocks into your mod 1 block by 1 block. Rather than delete your code, you can just disable specific lines that may be causing trouble. Figures 3-38 and 3-39 show you how to disable blocks.

When you have a bug you can't find, disable all blocks except the main function and the first block in the main function. Then run your mod. Then enable the next block, and run your mod. Continue doing that until you find the bug.

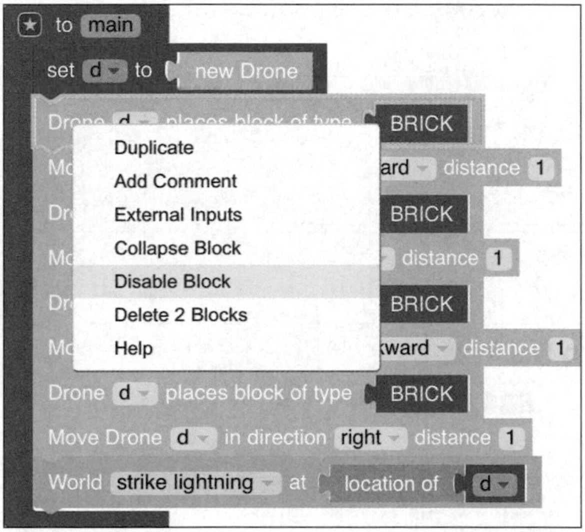

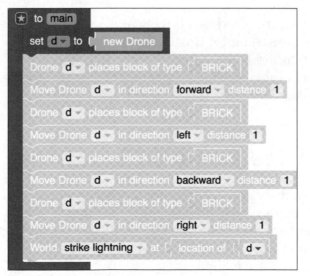

Figure 3-38

Figure 3-39

✔ **Ask for help in the forums.** LearnToMod has forums where you can ask for help, as shown in Figure 3-40. You can search by clicking on the magnifying glass or just browse topics to find them; Figure 3-41 shows a sample screen from a forum. Sometimes, someone else has already found the bug that you've run across, so the answer might even already be there.

Home	Mod	Learn	Classes	Social ⌄	log out

Forums

Published Mods

Un-Approved Comments ❶

Figure 3-40

LearnToMod

all categories ▸ | Latest | New (1) | Unread (1) | ★ Starred | Top | Categories   + New Topic

Topic	Category	Users	Posts	Views	Activity
★ 🔒📌 Welcome to the LearnToMod Forum Hi Modders, Parents, and Teachers! If this is your first time in the forum, Please read the following manifest prior to making any posts. Based on your feedback (and our own user experience with Forem), we've decided... read more			1	483	Dec '14

Figure 3-41

The term *bug* referred to a technical error even before computers were invented. Admiral Grace Hopper (an amazing computer scientist!) found a literal bug — a moth, to be exact — in one of the first computers, which was causing her program to misbehave.

Spawn Entities and Add Inventory Items

In the Inventory and Entity Commands badge set, you can find badges that show you how to spawn entities (for example, make creepers and cows appear) using drones and how to programmatically add objects to the inventory (make diamond swords or redstone appear).

Being able to spawn entities and add inventory items can be useful for preparing for nighttime in Survival mode in Minecraft or to protect yourself from other Minecraft players.

For example, you could create a tower and then use the drone to spawn a bunch of protective creepers around your tower, as in Figure 3-42.

> ★ function main
> set d ▾ to   new Drone
> Drone d ▾ spawns mob of type   EntityType creeper ▾

Figure 3-42

And you could arm yourself before nightfall by giving yourself a diamond sword, as in Figure 3-43.

To be able to give yourself the item, change the name in Figure 3-43 from Steve to *your* Minecraft username.

> ★ function main
> perform command   " give Steve diamond_sword "   for player   me

Figure 3-43

Build a One-Click House in Minecraft

In this section, I describe how to make a mod that builds a house. I like to refer to this process as building a one-click house, because whenever you're in Minecraft with one-click capability, you can have a house.

The following sections describe how to build a house in Minecraft. In the same way I show you how to build the tower, I tell you how to design, and then build, the house. This house can serve as a starting point for building a castle.

Start a new mod titled Simple_House, as shown in Figure 3-44.

Simple_House   ☐ Back   Actions ▾   Mod

◀ ▶ Minecraft
◀   Cloud
◀   Misc
◀   Logic
◀   Loops
◀   Math
◀   Text
◀   Lists
◀   Colour
◀   Variables
◀   Functions

Figure 3-44

Design a simple house on paper

First, sketch out the house on paper. (Figure 3-45 shows an example of how to do it.) Though this process is slightly more complicated than building the tower earlier in this project, in the "Build a Tower in Minecraft By Breaking Coding into Phases" section, the same principles of design apply, such as drawing at the house from multiple angles. As with the tower, you should figure out what functions are needed to build the house (see Figure 3-45).

In the Tower mod (described in the earlier section "Build a Tower in Minecraft)," you move code into functions as you write the mod; in this mod, you should decide what functions you want to create as you design the code. This alternative design strategy requires fewer refactoring iterations (the number of times you have to refactor your code) because you already know the functions, and you don't have to move code into functions *after* you write it. Figure 3-45 shows the functions labeled and defined on paper.

The drawings you create in the design phase don't have to be perfect. You just need to form an idea of what functions you need to write and how many blocks you need to place.

As with the Tower mod, write small bits of code and test them often. Before you even begin writing code, one strategy you can follow is to add all the functions you need in your mod. Figure 3-46 shows you how to do this, following the sketched-out design from Figure 3-45.

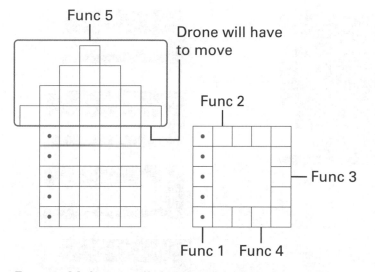

Func 1: Make a wall that is 5 blocks wide and
     5 blocks high
Func 2: 4 blocks wide, 5 blocks high
Func 3: 4 wide, 5 high
Func 4: 3 wide, 5 high

Figure 3-45

Write the first function for your house

Start with the first wall, the function named `wall_5x5`. First, make a line. Figure 3-47 shows the code for making a line of five bricks in one direction.

Then test your code. You see a scene similar to the one shown in Figure 3-48.

Sometimes, Minecraft worlds become so filled with trees that it's difficult to find a place to run mods with large structures in them. If this happens to you, just switch to Creative mode in Minecraft and run your mods in the sky. As long as you use material such as brick, your mods will appear in the clear, open sky around you. Though making structures in the sky becomes a problem whenever you want to use water or lava (because those materials will begin to fall), it also creates an amazing waterfall (or lavafall).

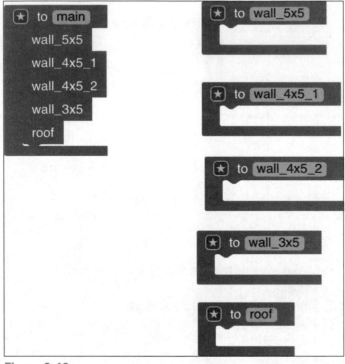

Figure 3-46

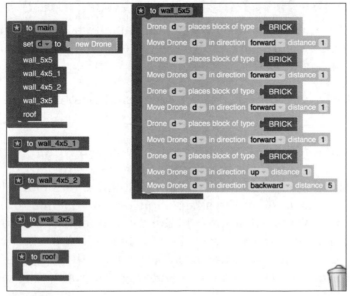

Figure 3-47

Figure 3-48

After you have one line of your house structure, you can easily extend it to five lines to make an entire wall. You can place a block and move the drone a lot of the time, as you did in to make the tower, or you can use loops.

A *loop* is a coding construct that you can use to repeat lines of code. You can use four types of loops in LearnToMod. Each one repeats the code that's inside of it. If you haven't done so already, go to the LearnToMod badges and complete all badges in the "Introduction to Loops" section to gain a basic understanding of loops.

Figure 3-49 shows you all the different types of loops you can use. In this case, you see how to use the loop that repeats a certain number of times, because you know that you want it to repeat exactly five times.

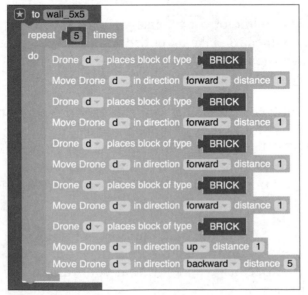

Figure 3-49

This loop repeats anything you put inside it; however many times you specify. Figure 3-50 shows your wall code using this loop.

Figure 3-50

Now test your mod. You see something like the scene shown in Figure 3-51.

Figure 3-51

Debug the first function for your house

If you run into a bug in the code (refer to Figure 3-51), never fear: You have debugging strategies. Debugging is an important skill to have, because rarely will you write code that is perfectly correct. You'll have to debug when you use LearnToMod or any other coding system, so I provide you with a few of my favorite strategies in the next few sections.

Identify the bug

Suppose that your mod has a lot of complex code in it. Not only does the mod have multiple lines, but they also repeat five times. Before you can find the bug, you should simplify the code.

Reduce the number of times the loop repeats. You know that one line works (refer to Figure 3-48), so try repeating two times, as shown in Figure 3-52.

Test your mod, and you see the scene shown in Figure 3-53.

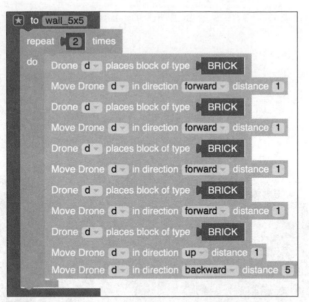

Figure 3-52

Figure 3-53

It seems that the second line is starting one block too soon, so the backward code is probably the bug.

Change the code and test it out (Debugging approach 1)

The bug is that the second line is off by one block. "Off by one" bugs are common in programming.

One way to fix the problem is to edit the line and test it. You know that the backward block is most likely the culprit, so change the backward block by 1, as shown in Figure 3-54.

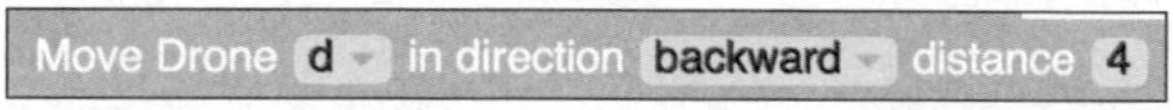

Move Drone d in direction backward distance 4

Figure 3-54

When you test your mod, you see that it works! It makes two lines directly on top of each other, as shown in Figure 3-55.

Commands Run
smesper

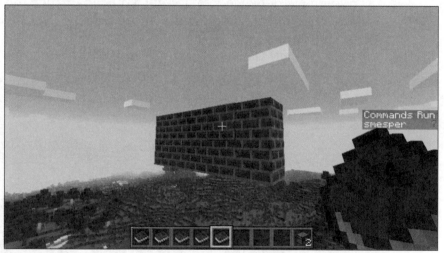

Figure 3-55

Use paper (Debugging approach 2)

Another way to debug is to trace the code. For each line of code, draw on paper what it does, such as drawing a red square when a brick block is placed. Then draw what you want to happen and look at the difference.

You can see in Figure 3-56 that what you have is moving backward five times, but what you need is to move backward four times.

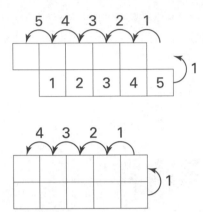

Figure 3-56

Complete the first function for your house

After you have debugged your code, you can change the loop back to iterating five times, and you see a scene like the one shown in Figure 3-57.

Figure 3-57

Prepare to write the second function for your house

Before writing the second function, you have to make sure that the drone is in the correct location. At the end of the first function, the drone moves up and back to the beginning of the line. Then the drone needs to reset to make the second wall appear in the correct place.

Write this reset code in the main function, as shown in Figure 3-58.

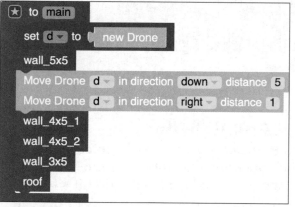

Figure 3-58

 When you work with any of the code in this project, make sure you have already completed the badges in the Functions, Drones and Locations, and Introduction to Loops categories. You can always revisit a badge you have already earned for a refresher, or even ask questions on the LearnToMod online forums if you're still having trouble.

Write the wall functions for your house

Write the second function as shown in Figure 3-59.

Continue to test and code until you have written all four functions to create the four walls of your house.

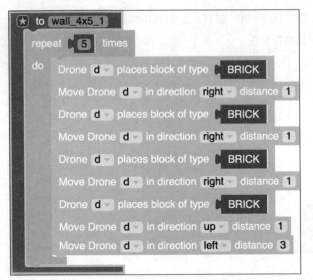

Figure 3-59

Sketch the roof function

The roof of your house is a pyramid, which is a bit tricky to make, so take out the paper and pencil for this one. You know that the base of the triangle should be 6 x 6 (so that it's one unit bigger than the house). Figure 3-60 shows one way to decompose the pyramid.

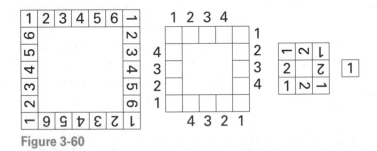

Figure 3-60

It looks like it might be useful to have a function for each of the drawings in Figure 3-60. Place functions for the roof, as in Figure 3-61.

to roof
6x6
4x4
2x2
to 6x6
to 4x4
to 2x2

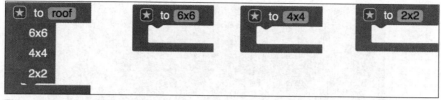

Figure 3-61

Write the functions for the roof

The 6 x 6 function is shown in Figure 3-62. It creates a square around the top of the house, as shown in Figure 3-63.

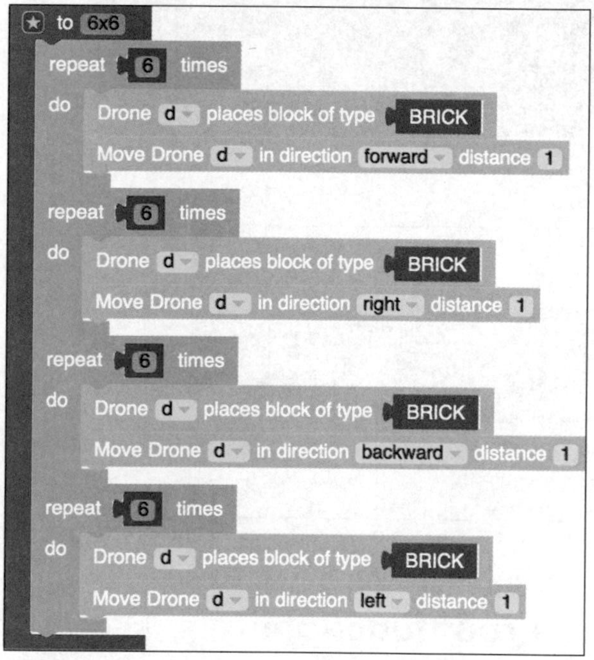

to 6x6
repeat 6 times
do
Drone d places block of type BRICK
Move Drone d in direction forward distance 1
repeat 6 times
do
Drone d places block of type BRICK
Move Drone d in direction right distance 1
repeat 6 times
do
Drone d places block of type BRICK
Move Drone d in direction backward distance 1
repeat 6 times
do
Drone d places block of type BRICK
Move Drone d in direction left distance 1

Figure 3-62

Reset the drone, as shown in Figure 3-64, and then write the 4 x 4 and 2 x 2 functions.

You can see the complete mod at `http://mod.learntomod.com/programs/sarah-Simple_House`.

Figure 3-63

Figure 3-64

Refactor the roof functions

After you have a completed house, you can refactor your code roof to make it simpler to understand.

Before you refactor, copy the mod and create another version of it named Simple_House_Refactored. That way, if you accidentally introduce new bugs, you can always revert to the original, working version.

The only difference between the three functions shown in Figure 3-65 is the number of times the loops repeat.

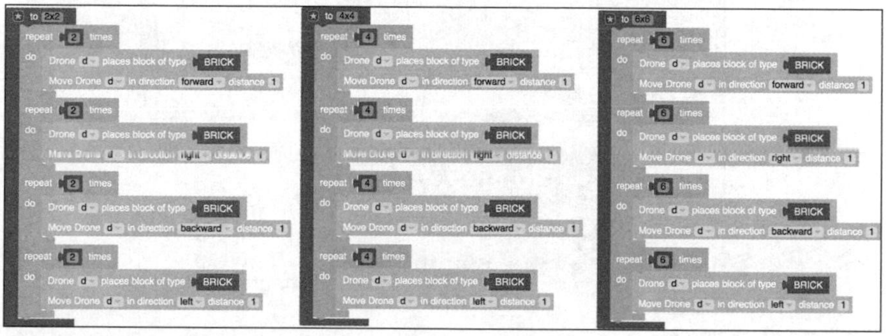

Figure 3-65

Rather than have three different functions, you can write one square function that takes a parameter named size.

A parameter is a kind of variable that can be used in a function to make it do something slightly different every time it's called. For example, if you have a function named jump, you could add a parameter named how_many_times. Then every time you call the jump function, you specify how many times it should make the character jump. The function still does the same thing (makes a player jump), but the slight change is that it jumps a different number of times (depending on what you specify). I tell you more about parameters when you reach the Parameters challenges in the LearnToMod software.

To make the square function, follow these steps:

1. Bring in a new function, name it square, and click on the blue star in the upper left corner, as shown in Figure 3-66.

2. Drag a new input into the square function, as shown in Figure 3-67.

3. Rename the input to become size, as shown in Figure 3-68.

4. Click on the blue star again to close the input dialog box, as shown in Figure 3-69.

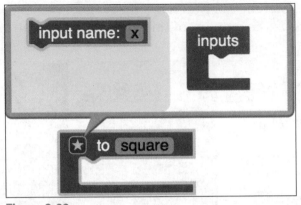

Figure 3-66

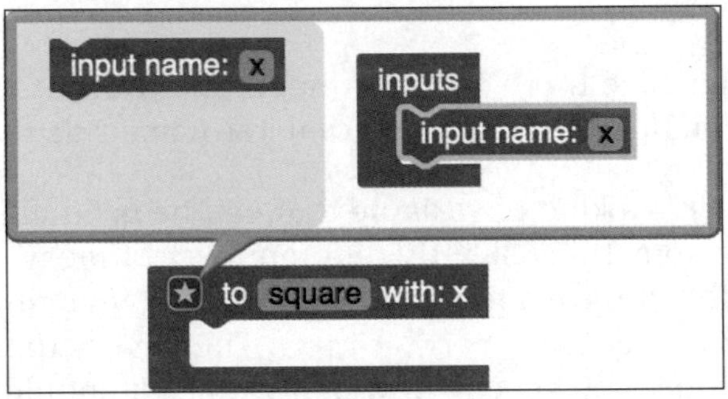

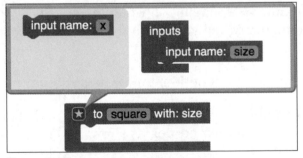

Figure 3-67

Figure 3-68

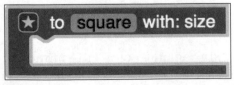

Figure 3-69

When you call the function, you specify the value for the parameter (see Figure 3-70) and then, throughout the function, the parameter (in this case, *size)* will have the specified value (in this case, 6). This allows you to call the same function, with different parameters, giving you slightly different outcomes, as shown in Figure 3-71.

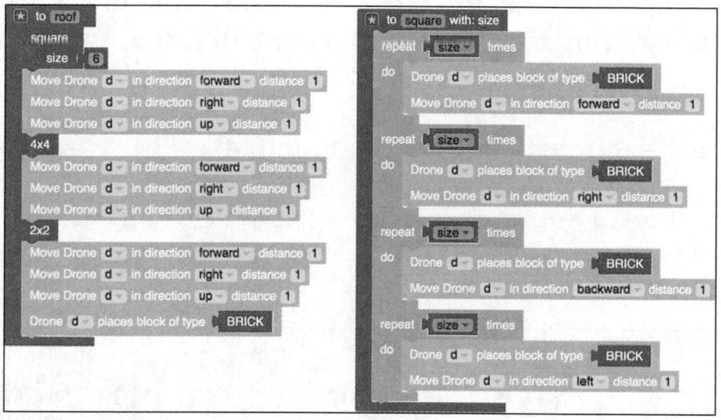

Figure 3-70

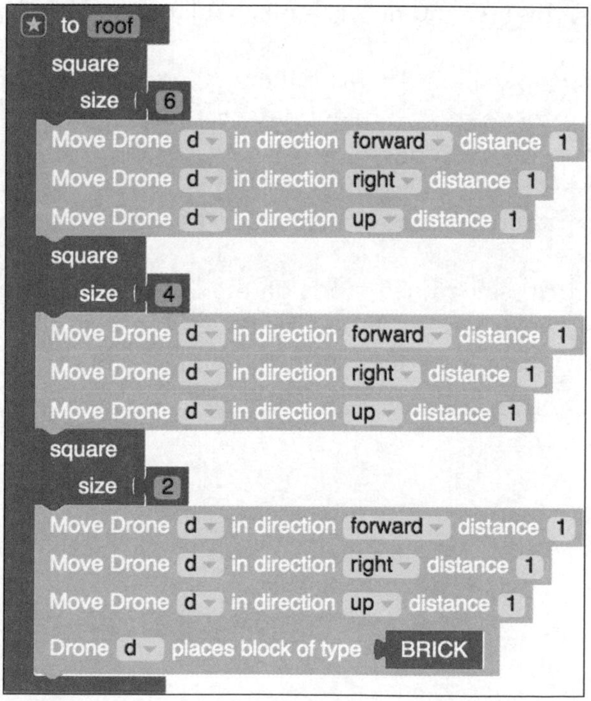

Figure 3-71

Inside the square function, put the four loops that are in the 2 x 2, 4 x 4, and 6 x 6 functions. Rather than loop by a certain number, loop by the parameter `size` (found under `variables`). Figure 3-70 shows how the square function should be written, and how you should call the square function from the main function.

You can replace the calls to the 4 x 4 and 2 x 2 functions with calls to the square function, just passing in a different value for the parameter size (refer to Figure 3-71).

The final refactored code can be found at

```
http://mod.learntomod.com/programs/sarah-Simple_
House_Refactored
```

Challenge yourself beyond this book

For a fun challenge, use the information in this project to build a large fortress with buildings, towers, and defense mechanisms.

Try to make at least four towers and three buildings, and try two different ways of protecting your fortress. You might have creepers at one entrance and lightning at another, for example.

Add in loops, or make patterns in your towers; don't always use brick.

Share your awesome fortress defense mods on the LearnToMod forums and with your friends. You can even invite friends into your server to check them out and try to get in by avoiding the defenses.

Part 2
Making Your First Minecraft Minigame

This week you'll build:

Making a Single-Player Game in Minecraft: Spleef

One of the most complex (but also fun!) Minecraft mods that you can make is a minigame inside of Minecraft. In this project, I guide you in making Spleef, a game in which a player walks around a platform and makes a block disappear by stepping on it. Using this simple idea, you can make a lot of variations of Spleef — for example:

- Players have to try to not fall into the lava that you have placed underneath the platform.

- After you put lava underneath the platform and other entities in the arena, players try to make the other entities fall into the lava before they do.

- In a game in which you've made multiple levels of platforms, players have to collect items on each level before they fall through to the level beneath them.

- In a multiplayer game, players have to try not to fall before the opposing player falls.

In this project, I show you how to make a simple Spleef game, and I give you tips on how to extend Spleef to make it your own.

Introduce the Gameplay Loop

Before you jump into making a game, even a simple one like Spleef, spend some time designing it so that you can prevent major errors when you go to develop it. As I mention in Project 3, you should always design your code before writing it. When you have a program that is complex, like a game, this rule becomes critical because it has so many pieces of code that could introduce errors. In this section I introduce you to the design technique known as the gameplay loop.

Figure 4-1 shows the basic gameplay loop with these four parts (as described in the following four sections):

✔ **Start:** Create a basic *scene* (the place where your game takes place).

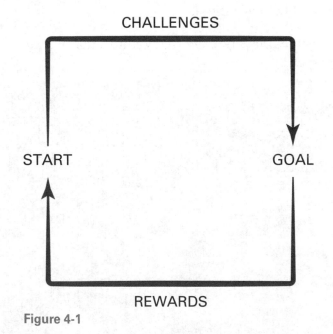

Figure 4-1

✔ **Goal:** Add a way to win and lose.

✔ **Challenge:** Make winning increasingly difficult.

✔ **Reward:** Make players want to win.

Start: Create a basic scene

Start by creating a basic scene for your game. You can begin by sketching out an idea on paper or by building it in Minecraft, without mods. The purpose of this step is to help you start thinking about the constraints that the scene will place on the players, and therefore on how the game will play out.

For example, making a game where you use the normal Minecraft world is much different from making a game where you're in a 20 x 20 arena with walls, because in the Minecraft world you have infinite space to play, while in the 20 x 20 arena you can only play in a 20 x 20 area. As you build and define the game, you can change the scene, such as make the arena bigger or add details. The design process is *iterative,* which means that you repeat each step multiple times. If you were building Minecraft from the ground up, you might start by creating a small world, but as you iterate through the gameplay loop, you make the world larger — eventually making it infinitely large, as it is today.

Coding takes iterations, so if you make a decision early on in your design, you can always make a change later.

Goal: Add a way to win and lose

Some of the games that you will want to make may be truly complicated, but if you break up the parts of the game according to the four gameplay loop pieces, you start to see that you can make a simple version of the game by creating only a basic scene and a way to win (or lose).

For example, if you were playing a super-simple version of Minecraft in Survival mode, the goal would be to not die at night. With only the Minecraft world and the goal to survive, it wouldn't be hard to survive, because there are no enemies. But at this point you would add the simplest feature to your game: the hearts. And you would add logic to the game to ask players whether they want to respawn whenever they run out of hearts. Again, at this point the game might not be much fun, but when you reach the next step (the challenge, followed by the reward), you start to add enemies and ways that players can earn back hearts.

Challenge: Make winning more difficult

Your game gets interesting when you start making it difficult for players to beat. At first, you might want to offer a small challenge. Don't worry: You can iterate up to the more difficult challenges as you cycle through the gameplay loop.

For example, in the simplified Minecraft game that I describe in the preceding section, the first challenge you might add is one creeper. You would put into the world one creeper that, upon seeing the player, tries to attack. This challenge makes the game more difficult than before because now the player can get hurt and lose a heart. This game might not be lots of fun, because players can only get hurt and can't defend themselves, but as you iterate through the gameplay loop, you can start adding more creepers — and even other creatures, and items for the player to use to defend themselves.

Reward: Make players want to win

Rewarding your players makes your game fun for them. Rewards can come in many forms, such as allowing players to move on to the next level or awarding them items such as stars and coins. Some games even take coins to another level, by allowing players to use coins to purchase items that can help them beat other levels.

In the example of a simplified Minecraft game (from the earlier "Goal" section), a player is rewarded with full health after finding an Instant Health potion. Similarly, if the player is playing Minecraft at the Peaceful difficulty level, simply staying alive and uninjured is rewarded with health.

Make Spleef: Iteration 1

After you know the basics of how to use the gameplay loop, you can begin to design and build a simple, single-player minigame using that technique. In this section, I show you how to make a game that you can play with friends, and you can even personalize it to make it unique.

First, make a new mod by following these steps:

1. Go to your home page and click Mod at the top of the page. Name the mod **Spleef**, as shown in Figure 4-2.

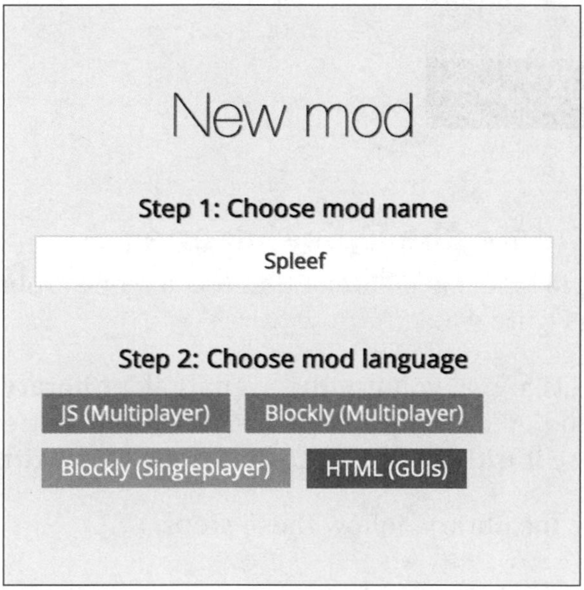

Figure 4-2

2. Click the Blockly (Multiplayer) button, and then click on the mod tile that gets created, as shown in Figure 4-3.

3. When the mod page opens, click the Code button to edit the code for the mod, as shown in Figure 4-4.

Now you're ready to make the Spleef game. In the rest of this section, I walk you through building on the gameplay loop.

Figure 4-3

Figure 4-4

Start: Create the Spleef scene

The scene in Spleef is an arena that has a fence around it, as you can see in Figure 4-5.

To make this arena, you use the ArenaBuilder library on LearnToMod. A *library* is a mod that is already written for you. You can use it without having to know how it is written.

To explore the library, follow these steps:

1. Go to `mod.learntomod.com/programs/sarah-ArenaBuilder`.

   You see these five functions:

   - `init`

   - `move_drone`

   - `ArenaWithFence`

   - `Platform`

   - `Fence`

Figure 4-5

2. Click the question mark (?) on each function.

A comment pops up, describing what the function does. For example, Figure 4-6 shows the comment for the Fence function.

3. Look through this code, and its parameters, to see what the code is doing.

Notice that there's no main function, because this mod cannot run on its own in Minecraft. Instead, it must be called from other mods, as explained in the following section.

Also notice the block: export. The export block, as you can see in Figure 4-7, makes the function that's written in the block accessible to other mods, meaning other mods can call the functions even though they're in a different mod.

Three functions are being exported: ArenaWithFence, init, and move_drone.

Now you can use these three functions in your Spleef game.

This function creates a square platform. The size is determined by the 'size' parameter. The 'height' parameter controls the height of the platform. The 'material' parameters controls what material the platform is made out of.

★   ?   function **Platform** with: size, height, material

repeat [size ▾] times
do   repeat [size ▾] times
      do   repeat [width ▾] times
            do   Drone **d** ▾ places block of type [material ▾]
                  Move Drone **d** ▾ in direction **up** ▾ distance **1**
            Move Drone **d** ▾ in direction **forward** ▾ distance **1**
            Move Drone **d** ▾ in direction **down** ▾ distance [width ▾]
      Move Drone **d** ▾ in direction **backward** ▾ distance [size ▾]
      Move Drone **d** ▾ in direction **left** ▾ distance **1**
Move Drone **d** ▾ in direction **right** ▾ distance [size ▾]

Figure 4-6

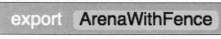

export   ArenaWithFence

Figure 4-7

Import the ArenaBuilder library

After you have exposed the ArenaBuilder library, go back to your Spleef mod and import that library. Follow these steps:

1. Under the Misc category, find the import block, as shown in Figure 4-8.

2. Drag it into the mod and type **sarah-ArenaBuilder** to replace the text lib-name, as shown in Figure 4-9.

   If you enter the mod name correctly, the block stays green and new functions appear under the Functions category, as shown in Figure 4-10.

   Notice that the three functions you now have access to are the three that were exported from the ArenaBuilder library.

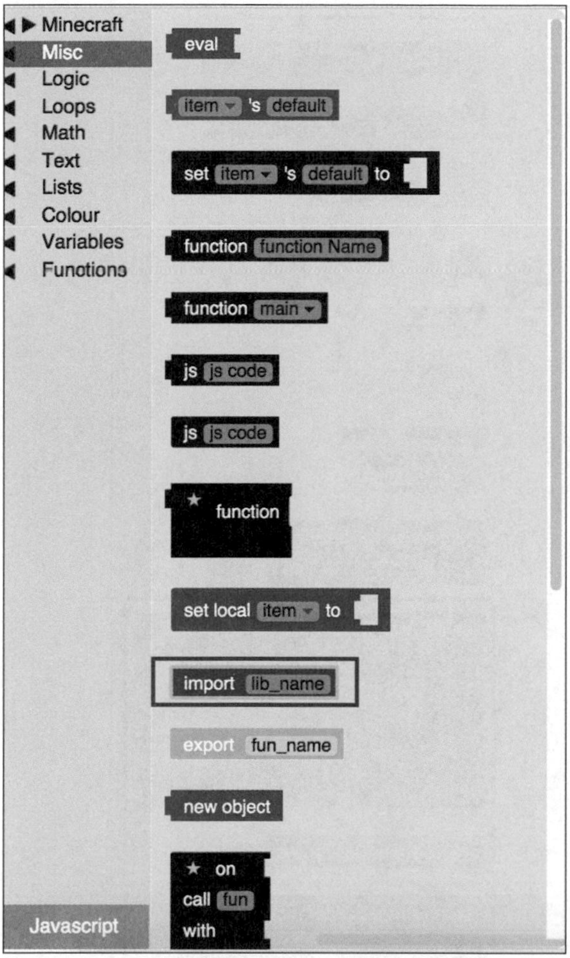

Figure 4-8

Figure 4-9

3. Create a main function, and add a call to the init function from the ArenaBuilder library.

The init function, if you look back at the library, basically creates the drone that will be used to create the arena for you. Figure 4-11 shows you how to set up your ArenaBuilder.

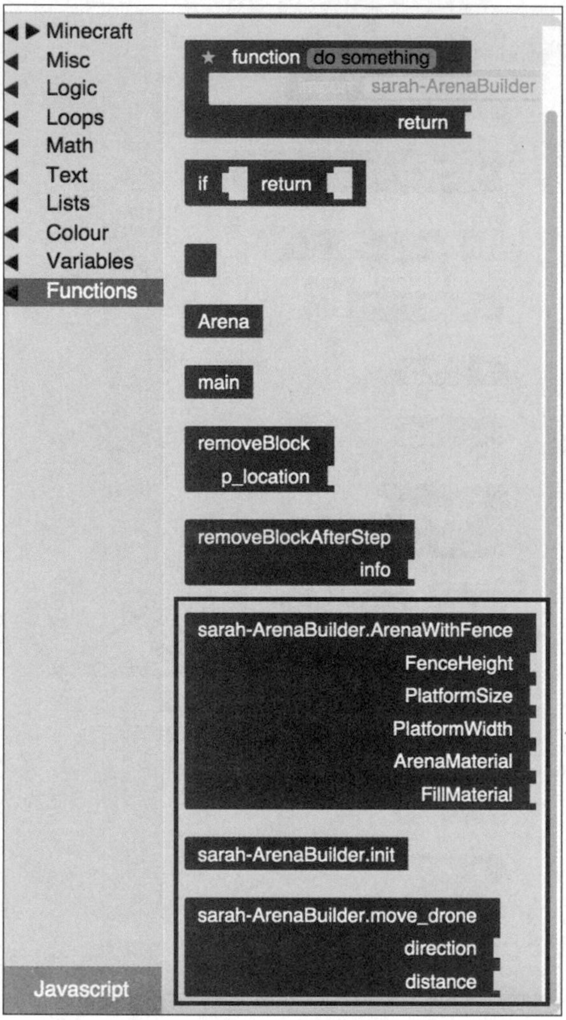

Figure 4-10

4. After your drone is ready to build your arena, add a call to the ArenaWithFence function from the ArenaBuilder library to the main function.

Figure 4-12 shows how to make a 20 x 20 arena made of diamond with a fence that's five blocks high and a platform width of one block. The arena will be filled with air. This makes the arena where you will play Spleef.

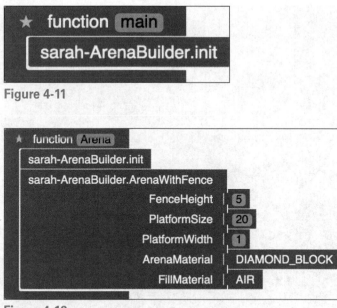

Figure 4-11

Figure 4-12

5. Even though you didn't write the ArenaBuilder library, test your code as you're building it. To test your code, make sure that the mod is saved, click the Mod button, and test the code in Minecraft.

   You see a scene like the one in Figure 4-13.

6. Before moving on to the goal in the next section, *refactor* the code — change it without changing what it does.

   In this case, you're refactoring the code so that the arena is built in a function named `arena` and so that the `arena` function is called from `main`. Figure 4-14 shows how to complete this step.

   Congratulations — you've created the basic Spleef scene!

Figure 4-13

Figure 4-14

Goal: Make a way to win and lose

After you have an arena to play in, you need to make a way for the player to win and lose. The easiest version of the goal for Spleef is this:

✏ **Win:** You win if you stay on the diamond platform.

✏ **Lose:** You lose if you fall through the platform.

It's impossible to lose now because players don't make blocks below them disappear. However, you can still code the logic for what happens if they fall through the platform.

Now you add in some basic logic to make sure that players start in the right place and know what to do when they respawn. Then, in the next section, I show you how to add to a challenge: Blocks disappear one second after being touched, making it possible to fall into the lava.

To set up the winning and losing conditions for Iteration 1 of Spleef, follow these steps:

1. Add a call to the ArenaBuilder's `SetArenaCenter` function at the end of the `Arena` function.

   The `SetArenaCenter` function will be in the Functions category of code because you imported my ArenaBuilder mod, and I exported the `SetArenaCenter` function so that you could use it.

   This step finds the center of the arena so that the player can be moved to the center for the start of the game. Figure 4-15 shows the added call to `SetArenaCenter` in the `Arena` function.

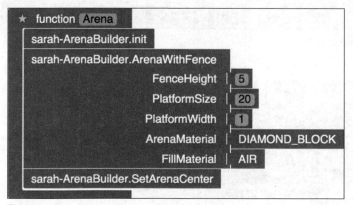

Figure 4-15

The `SetArenaCenter` not only finds the center of the arena but also creates a melon block in the arena. You use this melon block to start the game. The melon block is on the platform, as shown in Figure 4-16. Make sure you see it before moving on.

2. Make a new function named `StartGame` that takes `info` as a parameter, as shown in Figure 4-17. It's time to start the game when the player breaks the melon block.

The special function `StartGame` is used for events. You call it as shown in Figure 4-18.

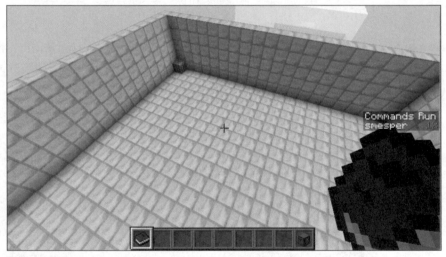

Figure 4-16

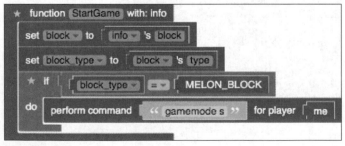

Figure 4-17

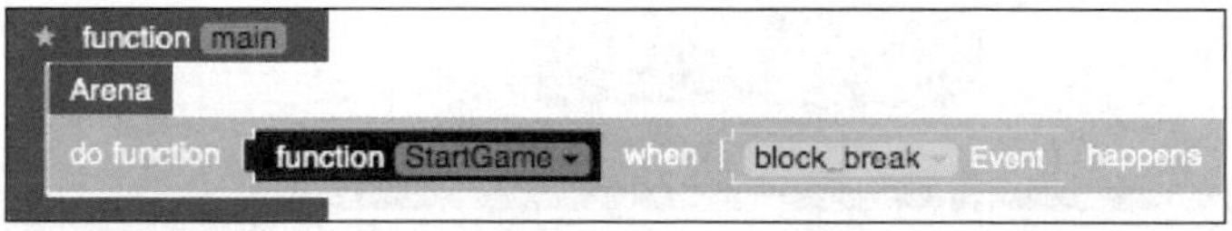

Figure 4-18

As you can see in Figure 4-18, the StartGame function is called only when a player breaks a block. So, every single time you break a block, this function runs.

However, you should put players into Survival mode only when the block they break is the melon block. Luckily, the info parameter represents the block you broke.

Variables are represented by a box consisting of two sections: name and data, as shown in Figure 4-19. Some variables are simple. As evidence, Figure 4-20 shows a variable named num with the data 5. Figure 4-21 shows a variable named name with the data Sarah.

<NAME>

<DATA>

Figure 4-19

Figure 4-20

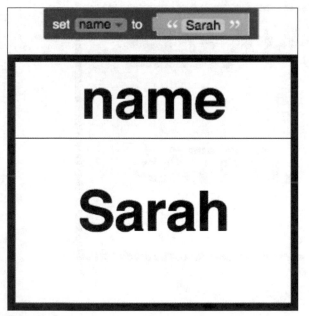

Figure 4-21

Some variables, on the other hand, are more complicated. For example, Figure 4-22 shows the info parameter for an event function associated with a block (that is, the block_break event). In Figure 4-22 you can see that the info parameter has a block for its data. The block has a type for its data, and the type's data is Melon Block.

The first two lines of code in the StartGame function follow the boxes shown in Figure 4-22 to find the type of melon block that was broken. Then you check to see whether the type that was broken was a melon block; if it was, you set the player's gamemode to Survival so that they have to step on the blocks and, possibly, lose all health if they fall through the platform.

3. Run the mod in Minecraft. When you break the melon block, you, the player, are put into Survival mode. Make sure the mod works before you continue.

4. Set up the respawn event.

Figure 4-22

A player who dies respawns to the center of the arena. This step is tricky: Figure 4-23 shows the SetupPlayer function, which is called when the player respawns; Figure 4-24 shows a way to call the SetupPlayer function when the player respawns.

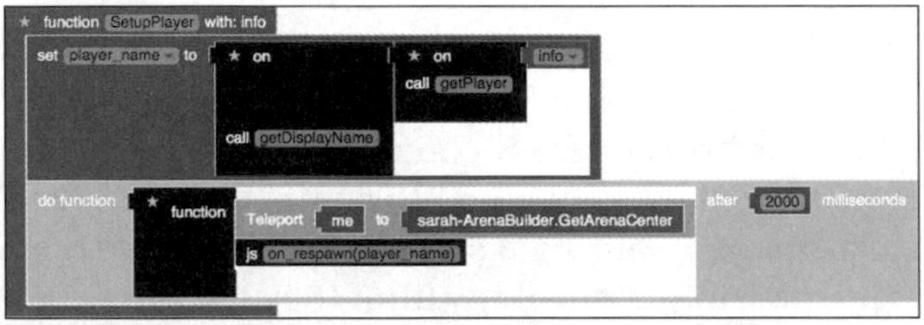

Figure 4-23

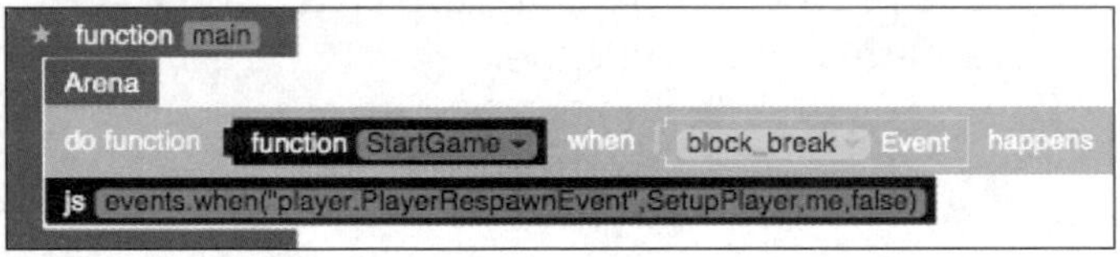

Figure 4-24

Take another look at Figure 4-23. The JavaScript block is used to call the event PlayerRespawnEvent, which requires these three parameters:

- The function to call when the player respawns.

- The player who is respawning.

- A true or false value that indicates whether this is a BedSpawn. (Use the false value because you don't want to teleport back to your bed.)

The SetupPlayer function gets data from the info parameter (refer to Figure 4-22) except that this time the info parameter is a player, not a block.

Figure 4-25 shows how this data is retrieved, and Figure 4-26 shows another way to get the same data.

Figure 4-25

After you have the name of the player, you can set up the event to teleport the player to the center of the arena, but only two seconds (2,000 milliseconds) after the player has respawned, as shown in Figure 4-26.

Events can be tricky. But you can always review badges you have already earned or ask questions on the LearnToMod forums if you need help.

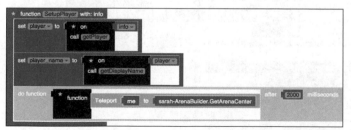

Figure 4-26

5. To test the mod, run it and break the melon block. When you do that, the gamemode should switch to Survival mode. Then break a diamond block and fall. Two seconds after you respawn, you're placed into the arena again.

You now have a game! The problem is that unless you actually break a diamond block, you never lose. In the next section, I help you find a way to make the game more challenging.

Challenge: Make blocks disappear one second after touching them

To add the first challenge to the game, you need to create another event. This time, when the player moves, a function is called that finds the location of the player and replaces, using an Air block, the block that is one block below the player's current location.

Figure 4-27 shows the two new functions you need to add — removeBlockAfterStep and removeBlock — and explains how to make a call to them from the main function.

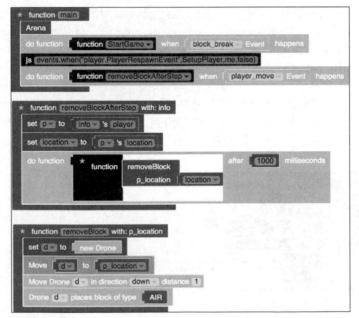

Figure 4-27

At this point, the entire Spleef mod should look like Figure 4-28, and you should test out the game.

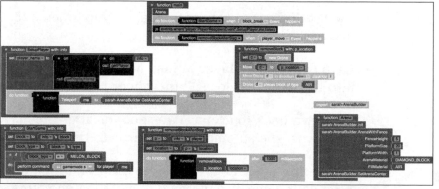

Figure 4-28

Test: Plan and execute test cases

Before playing your mod, identify the different test cases to make sure that your game is working properly.

> Test cases (as described in Project 3), are the different ways to test your mod to check whether it's behaving correctly.

Before you write a test case, make two lists that spell out

✔ **What you will test:** For example: Break the melon block.

✔ **What you expect to happen:** For example, the gamemode switches to Survival, and blocks below you disappear after one second.

If your test cases pass, you know that the mod is correct.

The following list shows five sample test cases for the Spleef mod:

✔ **The scene sets up properly.** When you run the mod, two arenas appear: a brick arena with lava and a diamond arena with a tall fence.

✔ **The player is put into Survival mode when the melon block breaks.** When you break the melon block, the player is set to Survival mode.

✔ **Blocks disappear.** One second after you touch a block, it disappears.

✔ **Lava causes the player to lose health.** When the player falls into the lava, they lose all their health.

✔ **Respawn back to arena.** Two seconds after the player respawns, she automatically returns to the arena again.

Come up with at least one more test case, and then test all of them on your game. If something doesn't match your expectation, such as blocks don't disappear when you walk over them, begin debugging the code, as explained in Project 3.

Debug: Fix bugs related to events

In Minecraft, you have no way to indicate that you no longer want to trigger events.

To *trigger* an event means that Minecraft recognizes that the event has happened and then calls the function that was set up in the event call. For example, earlier in this project, Figure 4-26 shows the `SetupPlayer` function, which has an event setup block in it. This event is triggered after two seconds, and then it teleports the player to the center of the arena.

Because you don't always want events to be triggered, testing your code can be difficult. For example, in Spleef you replace only the block below you with air if you're walking on diamond blocks (the arena).

If you run the Spleef mod and play it and then decide to explore a cave instead, you start to fall through the ground. That's because, as you can see in Figure 4-29, every 1 second the `removeBlock-AfterStep` function is called and the block below you is replaced with an air block.

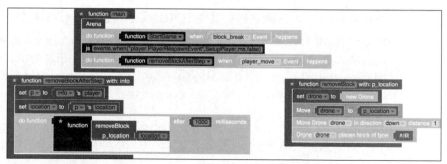

Figure 4-29

You can get an event to stop triggering, but you have to disconnect from the server and reconnect.

To avoid having to disconnect from the server every time you play a game of Spleef, you can add a simple conditional statement that checks to make sure that you're walking on a diamond block before it changes it to an air block.

Figure 4-30 shows the blocks you need to add to the remove-Block function to check the type of block you're walking on. This example is similar to the code I show you how to write for the StartGame function earlier in this project, in the section "Goal: Make a way to win and lose."

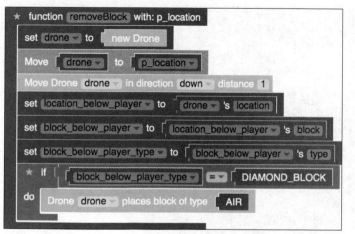

Figure 4-30

Reward: Reward the player with points

In the first iteration of the game, points can be represented by the number of blocks the player destroys before falling through the platform and dying. To make this happen, you just have to count the number of blocks that get converted to Air. Follow these steps:

1. Add to the StartGame function a new variable named blocks_destroyed that is set to 0, as shown in Figure 4-31.

2. Add 1 to the blocks_destroyed variable every time you place an air block in the removeBlock function, as shown in Figure 4-32.

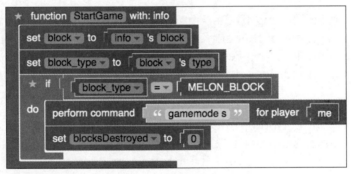

Figure 4-31

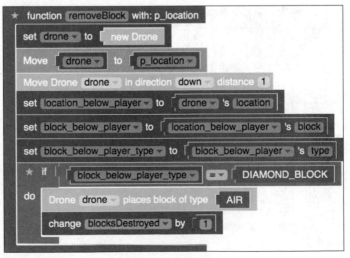

Figure 4-32

3. Add a `SendMessage` block to the `SetupPlayer` function to let players know how many blocks they have destroyed before falling through the platform, as shown in Figure 4-33.

When you play the Spleef game now, a message like the one shown in Figure 4-34 appears after you respawn.

Congratulations! You have completed an entire iteration of the gameplay loop for your Spleef game.

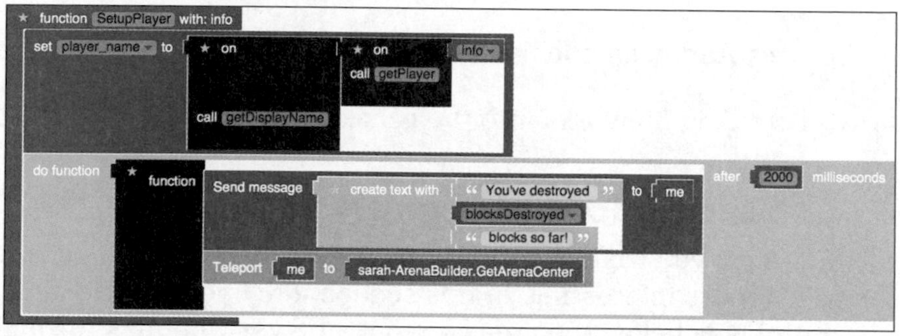

Figure 4-33

Figure 4-34

Make Spleef: Iteration 2

After you have completed an iteration of the Spleef game, you can repeat the gameplay loop and make the game more fun, challenging, and unique. In this section, I walk you through four examples in each of the parts of the gameplay loop so that you can

✔ Add a lava platform underneath the diamond arena.

✔ Challenge your player to destroy 200 blocks.

✔ Add in an enemy.

✔ Add fireworks into the game.

Start: Add a lava platform

After you have a working game, you can add to the scene to make it more interesting. In this section, I tell you how to add a platform of lava below the arena so that a player who falls through the platform falls into a lava pit.

Because you're using the ArenaBuilder library, the change to the Spleef code is minor. Figure 4-35 shows you what to call to add to the `arena` function so that you produce the scene shown in Figure 4-36.

Goal: Destroy at least 200 blocks

Because you're already counting the number of blocks that the player destroys as a part of the Reward phase in Iteration 1, you can easily add a bit of code to the `removeBlock` function to congratulate the player on becoming a Master Spleefer, as shown in Figure 4-37.

Challenge: Add an enemy

You can easily add an enemy into the arena by using the melon block as the spawning point. Figure 4-38 shows how to spawn a creeper in a random spot in the arena. Then the player has to

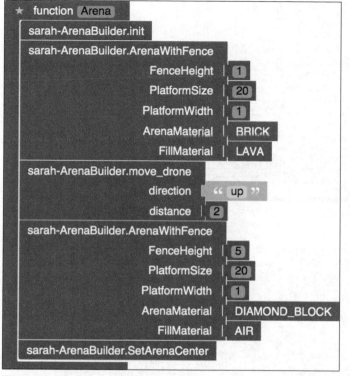

```
★  function  Arena
   sarah-ArenaBuilder.init
   sarah-ArenaBuilder.ArenaWithFence
              FenceHeight    | 1
              PlatformSize   | 20
              PlatformWidth  | 1
              ArenaMaterial  | BRICK
              FillMaterial   | LAVA
   sarah-ArenaBuilder.move_drone
              direction      " up "
              distance       | 2
   sarah-ArenaBuilder.ArenaWithFence
              FenceHeight    | 5
              PlatformSize   | 20
              PlatformWidth  | 1
              ArenaMaterial  | DIAMOND_BLOCK
              FillMaterial   | AIR
   sarah-ArenaBuilder.SetArenaCenter
```

Figure 4-35

Figure 4-36

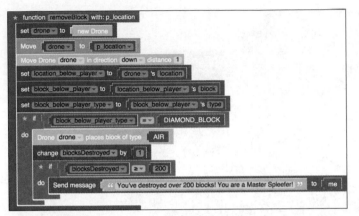

Figure 4-37

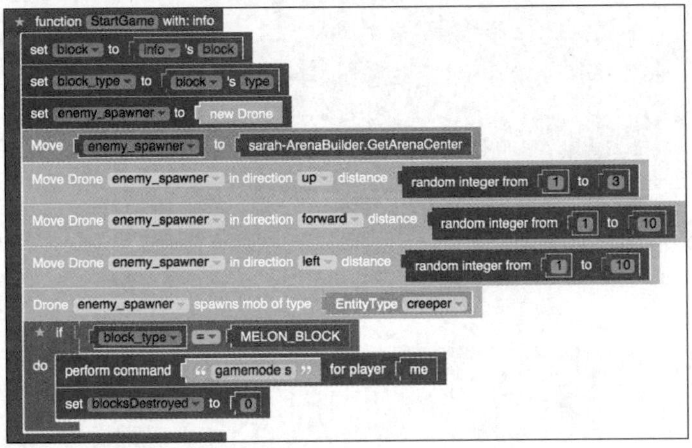

Figure 4-38

avoid the creeper *and* try not to fall before gaining at least 200 blocks. Figure 4-39 shows the player approaching the creeper.

Reward: Add fireworks

Finally, you can make the reward a little more interesting: Rather than congratulate players, you can give them a fireworks show! Figure 4-40 shows how to add the Fireworks block into the `removeBlock` function. You can find the `Fireworks` block under the World category, as shown in Figure 4-41.

Figure 4-39

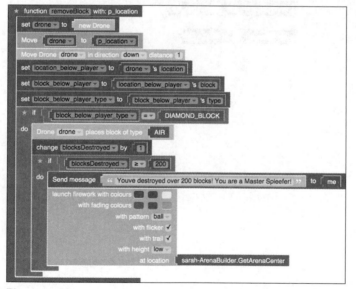

Figure 4-40

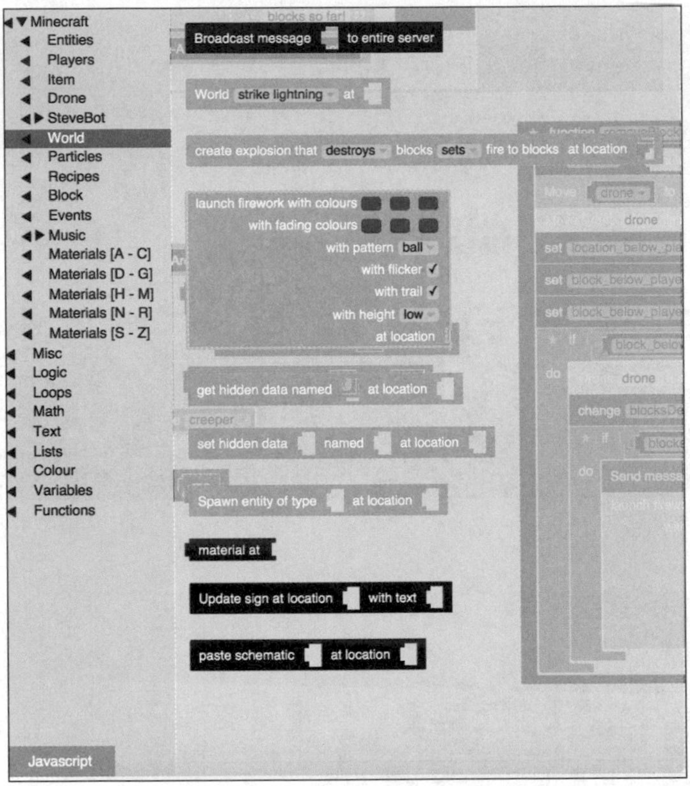
Minecraft
Entities
Players
Item
Drone
SteveBot
World
Particles
Recipes
Block
Events
Music
Materials [A - C]
Materials [D - G]
Materials [H - M]
Materials [N - R]
Materials [S - Z]
Misc
Logic
Loops
Math
Text
Lists
Colour
Variables
Functions
Javascript
Broadcast message to entire server
World strike lightning at
create explosion that destroys blocks sets fire to blocks at location
launch firework with colours
with fading colours
with pattern ball
with flicker
with trail
with height low
at location
get hidden data named at location
set hidden data named at location
Spawn entity of type at location
material at
Update sign at location with text
paste schematic at location

Figure 4-41

Challenge yourself beyond the book

After you have completed two iterations of the gameplay loop for Spleef, challenge yourself to either make a third iteration on the same game you build in this project or start over and make a new version of Spleef.

This time, you can make multiple arenas (as shown in the sidebar figure) and let the goal be to destroy at least 100 blocks on each level.

Making a Multilevel Minecraft Minigame: Monster Arena

Monster Arena **is a** multilevel Minecraft minigame in which the player is placed in a large arena with monsters that spawn around a melon block. The player's goal is to reach the melon cube without being attacked by the monsters. Every time the player reaches the melon cube, the moves on to the next level, with more monsters that are harder to defeat. The goal of the game is to reach the highest level possible before being defeated by the monsters.

In this project, I explain how to make a Minecraft mod that creates this game within Minecraft. Then you and your friends can play Monster Arena and see who can defeat the most monsters! Figure 5-1 shows you how the final game will look, with five creepers standing between you and the melon block.

Figure 5-1

Draw the Gameplay Loop

Before you begin coding your game, you must draw the gameplay loop for the Monster Arena game. Figure 5-2 shows the first iteration of the loop, as described in this list:

- ✔ Start: Build the arena

- ✔ Goal: Break the melon block

- ✔ Challenge: Add monsters

- ✔ Reward: Level up

In each iteration of the gameplay loop, you enhance each piece. To start out with, though, you have a simple arena with a melon block, 1 monster, and 1 level.

Iterate is a term from computer science that means "Do something over and over." And, more importantly, every time you do that something, you make progress. For example, if you iterate on the gameplay loop, you should add a feature, such as add a new challenge or a new reward, to your game in at least one place in the loop.

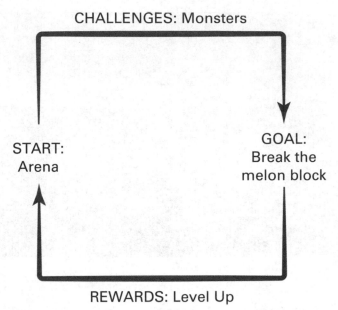

Figure 5-2

Iteration 1: Make Monster Arena

Here's one way to break up the iterations of the gameplay loop:

1. Start: Create a basic arena enclosed by a fence.

   In Monster Arena, the scene is a circular arena. A large fence surrounds the arena to keep the player and monsters inside it.

2. Goal: Add a melon block to break.

   In the Monster Arena game, you need to add a melon block in the arena, and you need to write code to reset the arena when the player breaks the melon block.

3. Challenge: Add monsters to the arena.

   In Monster Arena, you add one monster to the arena, and the player has to avoid the monster while trying to break the melon block. If the player successfully breaks the melon block, the game resets.

Ask your friends to test your game now. They'll probably say that it isn't much of a challenge to play, but you can gain insight into the kinds of challenges your players are looking for, such as more monsters or a bigger arena.

4. Reward: Replay the first level.

   In the first iteration of Monster Arena, the user breaking the melon block is the one who gets to play Level 1 again. In later iterations, you add more levels that the player gets to play.

   After you plan out the gameplay loop in Steps 1–4, it's time to build Monster Arena.

5. Make a new mod, and name it **Monster_Arena**. Choose Blockly (Multiplayer) as the language.

Start: Create a basic arena with a fence

When you build any game, the first thing you need is a basic scene for the game. For Monster Arena, you need a large, enclosed area. Figure 5-3 shows the kind of arena you build — a large, circular platform that has a radius of 20 blocks. Surrounding the arena is a fence, reinforced with stone. The fence is required so that neither the monsters nor the player can leave the arena throughout the game.

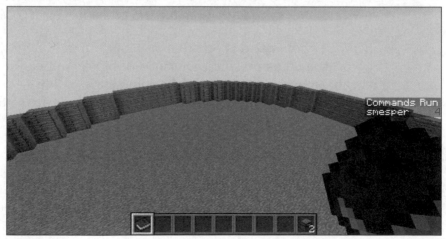

Figure 5-3

As you may have already learned in geometry class, the *radius* is the line from the circle's center point to any point on the circle's edge. Because everything in Minecraft is made with blocks, you count the blocks between the center and the edge of the circle, and that is the radius.

The initial scene is not the final version. You can always iterate on the design. The purpose of making the initial scene is to have a functional area to play the game and to keep gameplay inside this area. In Monster Arena, the player needs

✔ A place for the player and monster to run around

✔ A way to ensure that the monsters and player can't leave the area

For this basic scene, you create

✔ A platform

✔ A fence

In Project 4, in the section about making the first iteration of Spleef, I show you how to make an arena using the LearnToMod library named sarah-ArenaBuilder. This library makes square arenas, and this time you need to make a round one. Luckily, you can use WorldEdit commands to make the arena in LearnToMod!

A *WorldEdit* command is one that you can run in Minecraft to edit the world, such as making thousands of blocks appear at once. You can explore lots of WorldEdit commands online — search for the term *minecraft worldedit commands* using your favorite search engine.

Visit `http://wiki.sk89q.com/wiki/WorldEdit` (the official WorldEdit wiki) to see a list of all WorldEdit commands for Minecraft. Just click on one of the links to a category, like Filling Pits under Utilities to find the WorldEdit commands associated with filling pits.

To make the circular arena, you need to make a cylinder and a circle, which you can find under the Generation category on the wiki (it's toward the bottom).

Figure 5-4 shows how to use the WorldEdit commands in Minecraft. The WorldEdit commands use algorithms (another way of saying list of steps) to create the effect in the Minecraft world. The figure is from the wiki page about WorldEdit commands, found at

```
http://wiki.sk89q.com/wiki/WorldEdit/Generation#
    Cylinders_and_circles
```

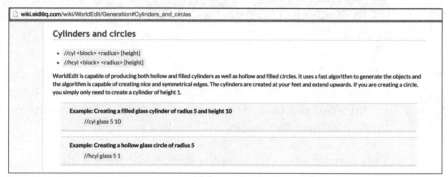

Figure 5-4

Test WorldEdit commands in Minecraft

Before writing the code to make the arena, test out the WorldEdit commands in Minecraft.

Figure 5-5 shows how to make a platform made of stone and with a radius of 20, and Figure 5-6 shows the platform that gets created.

Figure 5-5

Figure 5-6

When you're trying to build a large structure, double-click on the spacebar to hover, and then click and hold the spacebar to move up into the sky *before* running your mod. This action creates the large platform in the sky and makes it easier to see.

You can also test making the fence. Figure 5-7 shows how to make a stone fence. If you don't move, you can then give the command shown in Figure 5-8 to make a wooden fence inside the stone fence. It looks like Figure 5-9.

If you move after you have created the platform and before you create the fence, your fence won't fit perfectly around the platform. You can try it to see what happens: Run the platform command from Figure 5-5, and then move forward until you're near the center of the platform. Then run the command to create the fence, as shown in Figures 5-7 and 5-8.

```
//hcyl stone 20 4
```

Figure 5-7

```
//hcyl fence 19 4_
```

Figure 5-8

Figure 5-9

If you call all three of these WorldEdit commands without moving (refer to Figures 5-5, 5-7, and 5-8), you create an arena with a fence around it, as shown in Figure 5-10.

As I mention In Project 2, *calling* code means that Minecraft can handle that task.

Figure 5-10

Mod the arena in LearnToMod

After you have tested the WorldEdit commands, you can actually call them from the LearnToMod mod!

To call WorldEdit Commands from LearnToMod, you have to use a `PerformCommand` block, which can be found under the Players category, as shown in Figure 5-11.

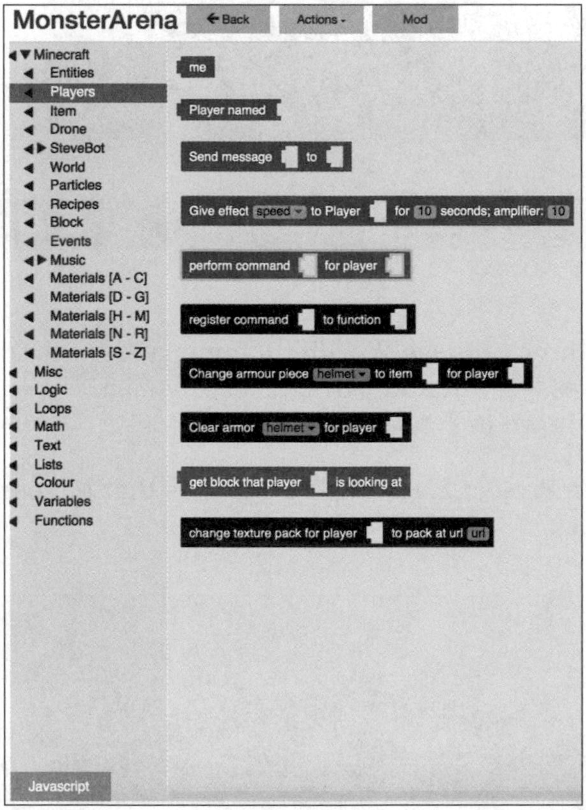

Figure 5-11

When you use a `PerformCommand` block, the first slash mark (/) is already included, so you need to have only one slash mark to make the platform and fences. Figure 5-12 shows you what the `main` function looks like for the initial scene.

Test your mod to make sure that the result is the same kind of arena shown in Figure 5-10.

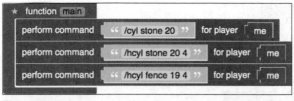

Figure 5-12

Refactor: Move the arena code to a new function

Before you move on to adding a goal, refactor your code so that the main function stays simple. Figure 5-13 shows you how to refactor your code to clean up the main function.

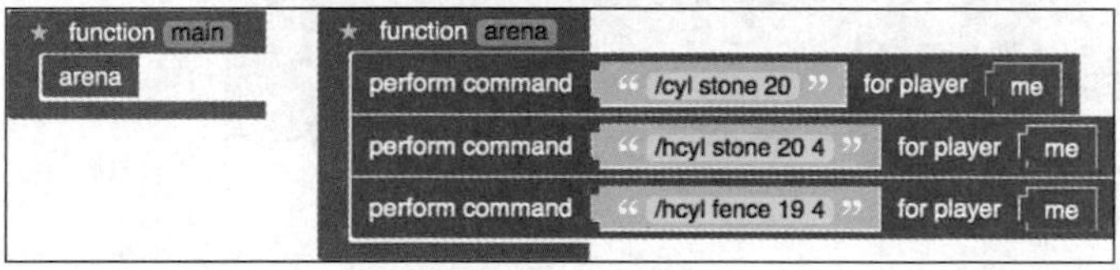

Figure 5-13

Goal: Add a melon block to break

After you have set up the initial scene, you can use the scene for a game. The arena function stays the same, but you add a melon block on the opposite side of the arena from the player.

Figure 5-14 shows the new function, SetupGame, which creates the arena, places the melon block, and puts the player in the starting position.

To add a melon block, follow these steps:

1. Create the SetupGame function and add a call to SetupGame to main.

2. Add a new drone named d and move it to one side of the arena. The drone should move only 18 blocks because the stone and the fence occupy 2 of the blocks and you want the player to be inside the fence.

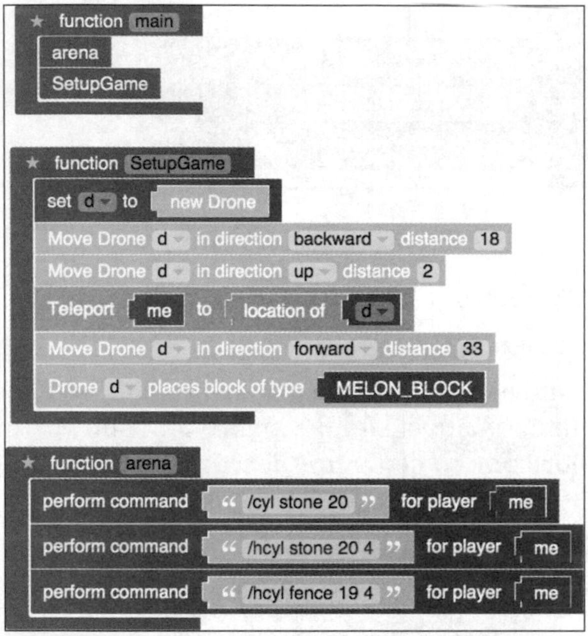

Figure 5-14

3. Move the drone up by 2 so that the player starts above the platform and falls into the arena.

4. Move the player to the location of the drone. Now the player is at the starting position.

5. Move the drone to the opposite side of the arena. Moving the drone 33 blocks leaves 2 blocks empty between the melon block and the fence.

6. Place the melon block and move the drone backward by 1 block.

At this point, nothing happens when the player breaks the melon block, and you write that code in Iteration 2.

Test: Make sure your game is set up correctly

In the previous section, you make specific calculations to ensure that the player and the melon block are on opposite sides of the arena. Now test your mod. Figure 5-15 shows the scene you see when you run the mod, and Figure 5-16 gives you the bird's-eye view.

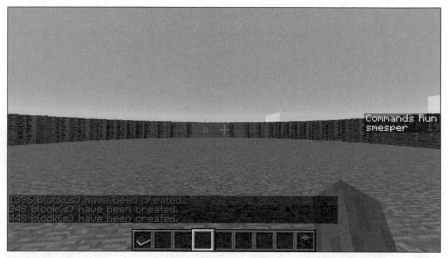

Figure 5-15

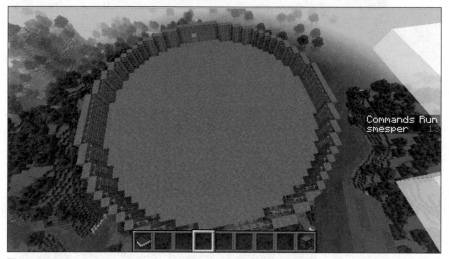

Figure 5-16

Challenge: Add monsters to the arena

After you have your game all set up, you can start making it playable. On the first iteration of the gameplay loop, you should add one monster for the player to defeat, or to at least get around. This time, write the code to spawn the monster in a separate function from the beginning.

Figure 5-17 shows the code you need to add to make 1 monster spawn near the melon block. Note that before you spawn the creeper, you move the drone 1 block away from the melon block so that the creeper doesn't spawn inside the block and immediately die.

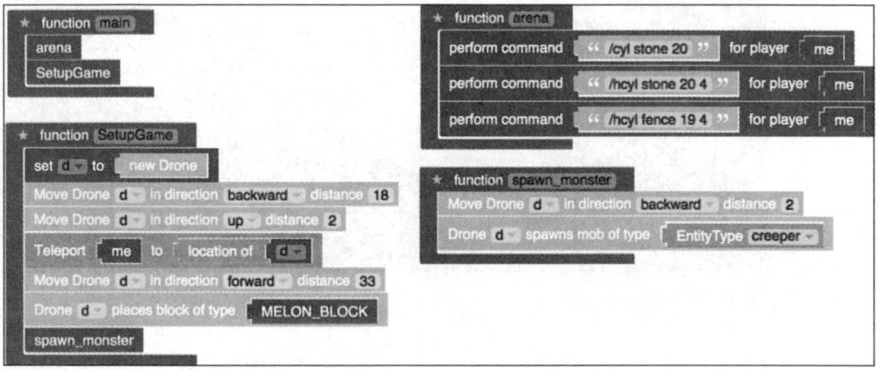

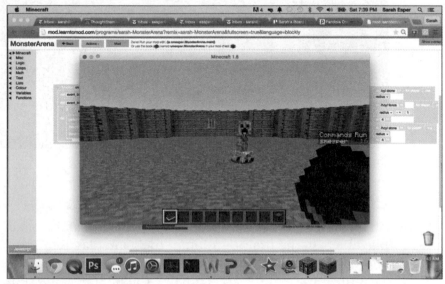

Figure 5-17

Now when you test your game, you see a screen similar to Figure 5-18.

Figure 5-18

Reward: Replay the first level

In future iterations of the gameplay loop, you reward players with levels that are more difficult to complete. For this first iteration, however, just let people replay the first level.

To do this, you have to make an event (as described in Project 4) that calls the function on_block_break whenever the player breaks any block. Figure 5-19 shows how to add this *event call* into the main function.

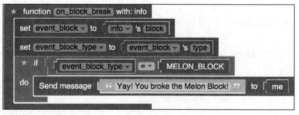

Figure 5-19

The on_block_break function checks to see whether the melon block was the block that was broken. If it was, you see the message "Yay! You broke the Melon Block!" Figure 5-20 shows the on_block_break function.

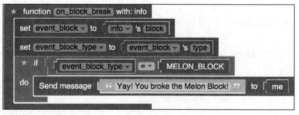

Figure 5-20

In addition to congratulating the player for breaking the block, you want that person to restart the level. To do this, you add two variables to the SetupGame function: one that keeps track of where the player should start out and one that indicates where the melon block should be placed. Figure 5-21 shows how to add these two variables.

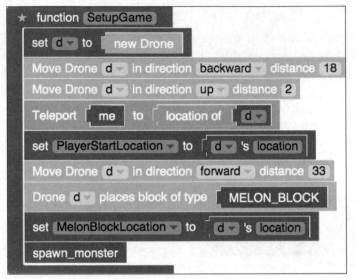

Figure 5-21

Now you can write a ResetGame function that

✔ Destroys all monsters in the arena

✔ Teleports the player back to the starting position

✔ Moves Drone d back to the melon block's starting position

✔ Places a new melon block

✔ Spawns monsters again

Figure 5-22 shows this new function, and Figure 5-23 shows how to call it from the on_block_break function.

Test: Iteration 1 completed

After you have completed the four parts of Iteration 1, you can test your game and make sure that everything is working correctly. Your code should look just like Figure 5-24.

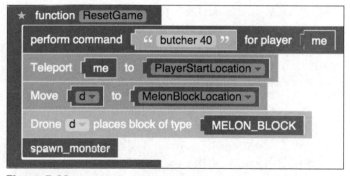

function ResetGame

perform command " butcher 40 " for player me

Teleport me to PlayerStartLocation ▾

Move d ▾ to MelonBlockLocation ▾

Drone d ▾ places block of type MELON_BLOCK

spawn_monster

Figure 5-22

function on_block_break with: info

set event_block ▾ to info ▾ 's block

set event_block_type ▾ to event_block ▾ 's type

★ if event_block_type ▾ = ▾ MELON_BLOCK

do Send message " Yay! You broke the Melon Block! " to me

ResetGame

Figure 5-23

function main

arena
SetupGame
do function function on_block_break ▾ when block_break ▾ Event happens

function SetupGame

set d ▾ to new Drone
Move Drone d ▾ in direction backward ▾ distance 18
Move Drone d ▾ in direction up ▾ distance 2
Teleport me to location of d ▾
set PlayerStartLocation ▾ to d ▾ 's location
Move Drone d ▾ in direction forward ▾ distance 33
Drone d ▾ places block of type MELON_BLOCK
set MelonBlockLocation ▾ to d ▾ 's location
spawn_monster

function arena

perform command " /cyl stone 20 " for player me
perform command " /hcyl stone 20 4 " for player me
perform command " /hcyl fence 19 4 " for player me

function on_block_break with: info

set event_block ▾ to info ▾ 's block
set event_block_type ▾ to event_block ▾ 's type
★ if event_block_type ▾ = ▾ MELON_BLOCK
do Send message " Yay! You broke the Melon Block! " to me
ResetGame

function ResetGame

perform command " butcher 40 " for player me
Teleport me to PlayerStartLocation ▾
Move d ▾ to MelonBlockLocation ▾
Drone d ▾ places block of type MELON_BLOCK
spawn_monster

function spawn_monster

Move Drone d ▾ in direction backward ▾ distance 2
Drone d ▾ spawns mob of type EntityType creeper ▾

Figure 5-24

When testing, develop a series of test cases and predictions so that you can make sure everything that you've written has been tested (see Project 4, the section about planning and executing test cases).

Iteration 2: Add Levels

On the second iteration of the gameplay loop, you can add more levels to your game. You can also take this time to make the arena more unique and personalized, or change the item you make the player break to go on to the next level.

Start: Make the arena unique

Add some designs to the arena floor. In Figure 5-25, you can see where I used two `//hcyl` WorldEdit commands to make one hollow cylinder of glass and one of diamond. You can see the changed arena function in Figure 5-26.

Take the time to be creative and to make your own design in either the platform or the fences. You might even want to add a ceiling to the arena!

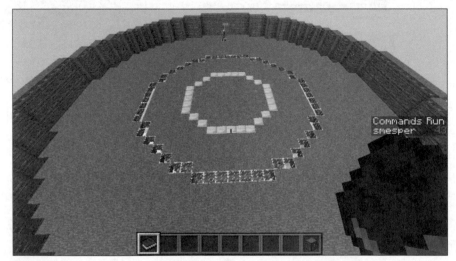

Figure 5-25

★ function arena		
perform command [`" /cyl stone 20 "`] for player	me
perform command [`" /hcyl glass 10 "`] for player	me
perform command [`" /hcyl diamond 5 "`] for player	me
perform command [`" /hcyl stone 20 4 "`] for player	me
perform command [`" /hcyl fence 19 4 "`] for player	me

Figure 5-26

REMEMBER

If you add a ceiling, start your player inside the arena. Otherwise, that person will get locked out.

Goal: Wait until a later iteration

Sometimes, when you're iterating through the gameplay loop, you don't want to make a change in one of the sections, such as when your goal is still the same (to break a melon block), so you don't need to change anything in the Goal section. No problem.

On Iteration 2, you still might want the goal to be to break the melon block, so you don't have to make any changes to the goal this time around.

Challenge: Add monsters

Maneuvering around one creeper isn't too difficult. On Iteration 2, you should add more monsters that the player has to avoid and still break the melon block. By making one small change to the spawn_monster function (see Figure 5-27), you can spawn 5 creepers instead of 1.

```
★ function  spawn_monster
    Move Drone  d ▾  in direction  backward ▾  distance  2
    repeat  5  times
    do    Drone  d ▾  spawns mob of type  [ EntityType  creeper ▾ ]
```

Figure 5-27

Figure 5-28 shows how the game becomes more challenging with more creepers blocking the melon block.

Figure 5-28

Reward: Add a second level

In Monster Arena, levels are differentiated by which monsters the player faces. To add a second level, the first thing you have to do is create a variable named Level that keeps track of which level the player is on. This variable should start at 1 because the player starts on the first level.

You should also create a list of monsters. Name the list Monsters and add two types of monsters: creepers and zombies.

Figure 5-29 shows how to create these two variables in the SetupGame function.

Now that you have a list of monsters to choose from, you can change the spawn-monster function to choose which monsters to spawn, based on the level the player is on. Figure 5-30 shows how to choose the correct item from the list.

Finally, you have to increase the level variable every time the player breaks the melon block. If the player reaches the final level (which is now Level 2), notify her that the game is finished; otherwise, the game should reset, but with the new monsters.

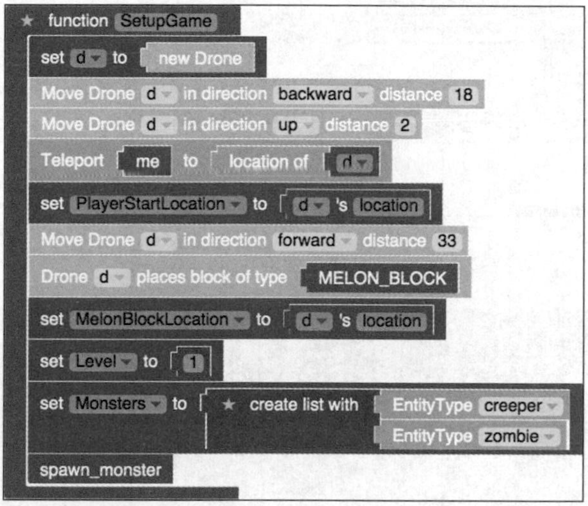

Figure 5-29

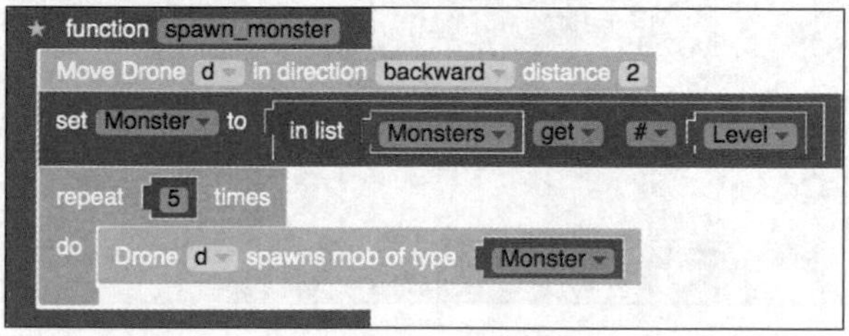

Figure 5-30

Figure 5-31 shows the changes to on_block_break that need to happen to start the new level.

Test: Make sure both levels work

After you have added the changes to the spawn-Monster function, test your mod. When you start the test, you should see five creepers, as shown in Figure 5-32.

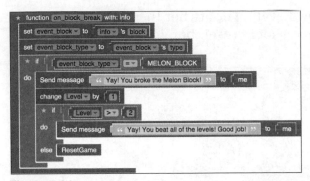

Figure 5-31

Figure 5-32

If you break the melon block, the game resets and you see five zombies, as shown in Figure 5-33.

If you break the melon block again, the game doesn't change, but you see the message "Yay! You beat all of the levels! Good Job!" (see Figure 5-34).

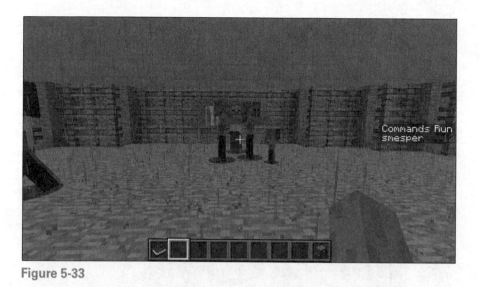

Figure 5-33

Figure 5-34

Iteration 3: Add Even More Levels and Challenges

After you start getting the hang of making the Monster Arena minigame, it shouldn't be too hard to add a few more levels and challenges.

In this iteration, you can skip the Start and Goal sections, described earlier in this project, because the game is becoming fun simply by adding more challenges and rewards.

Challenge: Switch to Survival mode

You may have noticed that a player can pretty easily advance past all the creatures, because the player is in Creative mode. As you did in Project 4, you should add a `PerformCommand` block so that when the game starts, the player is put into Survival mode (refer to Figure 4-17).

Figure 5-35 shows the changes you make to the `SetupGame` function to do this.

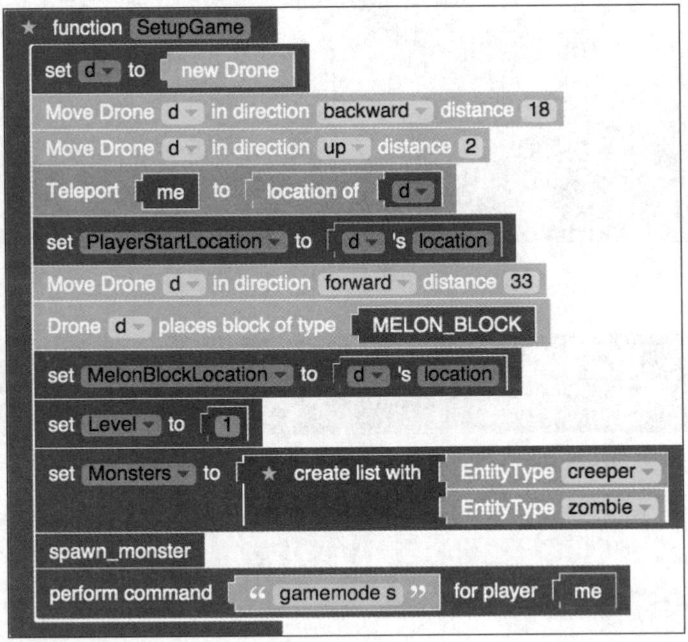

Figure 5-35

Now that you've made it easier for the player to die, you should also include an event to be triggered whenever the player respawns. Figure 5-36 shows the changes to the `main` function and the new `RespawnPlayer` function to teleport the player back to the arena.

Reward: Add five more levels

Adding levels is pretty easy because you have already set up the levels to be based on a list.

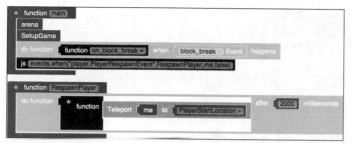

Figure 5-36

First, refactor the on_block_break function to confirm that you have iterated through all of the monsters in the Monster list, and not a specific number (like 2). Figure 5-37 shows how to change the conditional statement to have it based on the list length.

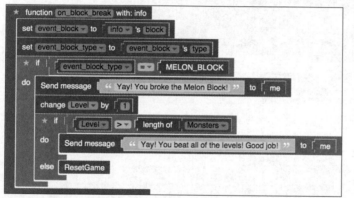

Figure 5-37

Now you can just add more monsters to your monster list. Figure 5-38 shows the updated SetupGame function.

Finally, you can change the spawn_monster function, shown in Figure 5-39, to spawn more monsters as the levels become more challenging.

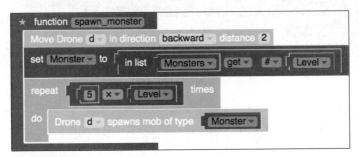

Figure 5-38

Figure 5-39

Make More Iterations: Be Creative and Unique

After you have created a fully functional, multilevel Monster Arena minigame, you can continue iterating on the gameplay loop to make even *more* challenges and rewards and to set different goals.

You can even make the arena more unique, such as adding patterns to the platform, as you can see in Figure 5-1.

A more challenging enhancement is to add random monsters at each level. For example, at Level 1 you add 5 creepers, and at Level 2 you add a total of 10 monsters that are (randomly) creepers or zombies. At Level 3, you add a total of 15 monsters that are (randomly) creepers, zombies, or spiders. Figure 5-40 shows how to add randomness to the spawn_monster function.

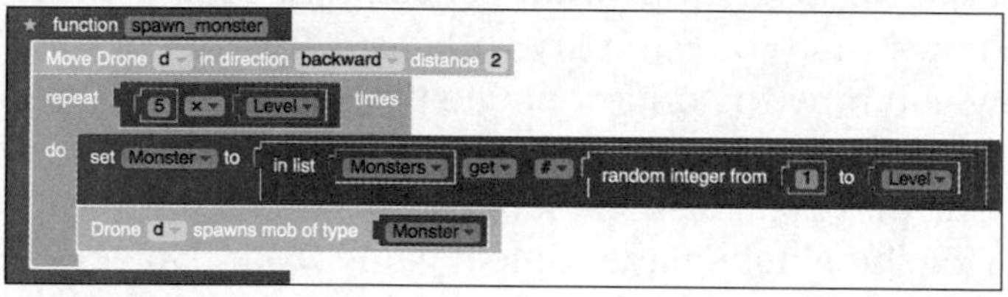

Figure 5-40

Minecraft Modding with Friends: The Multiplayer Version of Spleef

Making Minecraft minigames can be a lot of fun because after you make it you can play games inside of Minecraft for hours, but what is even more fun is making minigames that you can play with your friends. In this project, I show you how to convert single-player games (games that only have player) into multiplayer games (games that have more than one player). I also explain how to change the gameplay loop (for the single-player Spleef game from Project 3) so that you can design a multiplayer game from the ground up.

Start from the Single-Player Spleef Game

Rather than remake the entire Spleef game, you can start from the single-player version and turn it into a multiplayer version.

Note: Before you begin this section, you should have already built Spleef. If you haven't built it yet, go back to Project 4 and build a single-player Spleef game.

To start from single-player, follow these steps:

1. Open the completed single-player Spleef mod (described in Project 4), click the Actions tab, and then choose Copy from the menu, as shown in Figure 6-1.

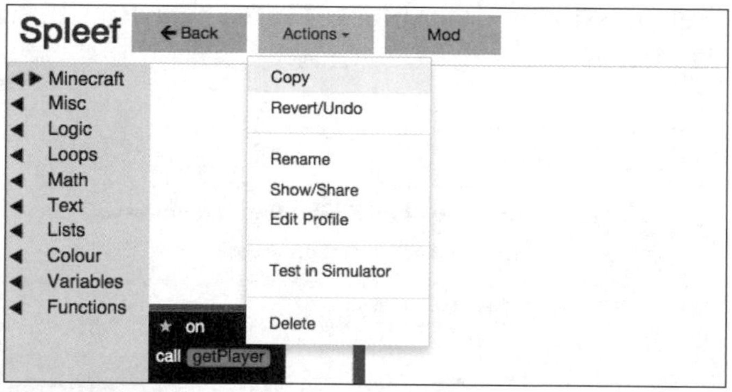

Figure 6-1

2. Click to select the copied version of Spleef, shown in Figure 6-2, and then click on Code to go into the programming environment.

Figure 6-2

3. At the top of the screen, click the Actions tab and choose Rename from the menu, as shown in Figure 6-3.

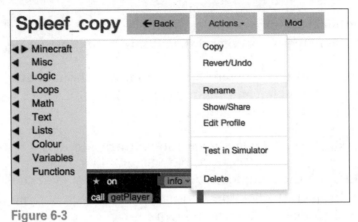

Figure 6-3

4. Rename the mod to **Spleef _Multiplayer**, as shown in Figure 6-4.

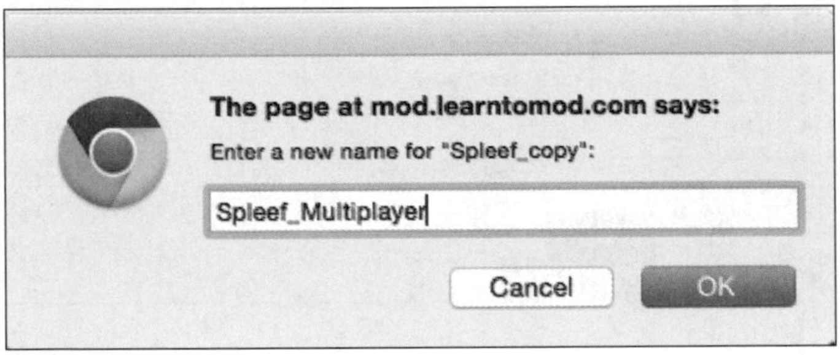

Figure 6-4

5. After the page reloads, click on the Spleef multiplayer mod again, as shown in Figure 6-5, and then click the code button to go into the programming environment.

Now you're ready to start modifying your single-player version of Spleef to make it multiplayer.

If you make a mistake at any point, you can always go back and make another copy of your single-player version.

"Spleef Multiplayer" by sarah (Multi)

Figure 6-5

When an expert modder decides to use an earlier version of a chunk of code, it's called *reverting*. This is why you should always test your code as you're writing it, to avoid making a single tiny mistake *just* before you finish making your multiplayer game and then being unable to figure out how to undo it. On top of all that, you have to revert to the single-player version and start over.

Test, and test often!

Summarize the Gameplay Loop

Even though you're making a multiplayer game, you can still use the gameplay loop to guide you in making small changes. At each iteration, you can test to ensure that you haven't made any mistakes. This makes reverting to earlier versions easier because you're making only small, incremental changes, and because they're small, they're easier to undo.

The gameplay loop (see Project 4) is shown in Figure 6-6.

Before you start iterating on the gameplay loop, summarize on paper the changes you plan to make, like this:

- ✔ **Start:** No changes need to be made to the scene yet, unless you want to enlarge the arena to make the games last longer.

- ✔ **Goal:** The new goal is to break 200 blocks before your opponent does.

✔ **Challenge:** The new challenge is adding a player to the scene.

✔ **Reward:** The new reward is beating the other player.

Figure 6-6

The new gameplay loop should be simple and not have a lot. After you successfully make the multiplayer game, you can always revisit the gameplay loop and make it more interesting, such as making the arena bigger.

Iteration 1: Refactor the Single-Player Version

Before you add a second player to the game, you need to do a bit of refactoring. Instead of referring to me, you should refer to a specific player who is defined in your mod. In this section, I walk you through the steps to do it — while setting up for the multiplayer version.

Why would you start making your game multi-player by only replacing me rather than also including Player2? When you make a lot of changes to your code to refer to a player by name, rather than use the me block, you can test the changes you made before adding even more complexity with multiple named players. In Iteration 2, you add in Player2.

First you need to determine the Minecraft username of Player1 and put that info into your mod. Follow these steps:

1. Make a new function named **SetupMultiplayer**, and call it from main, as shown in Figure 6-7 (and described in Project 2).

Figure 6-7

The main function already has other blocks in it because you're starting from the Spleef game I show you how to build in Project 4.

2. Create a new variable named **Player1**, and set it to the first player's Minecraft username, as shown in the example in Figure 6-8. In this example, I'm using thoughtstem as Player1.

Figure 6-8

3. Review your mod and replace any references to me with references to the player with the name of the Player1 variable.

For example, if your Minecraft name is thoughtstem, Figure 6-9 shows three ways that you can reference your player in Minecraft.

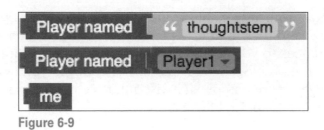

Figure 6-9

Start with main (as shown in Figure 6-10) and step through it line by line. This means you will look at the functions when they are called from main.

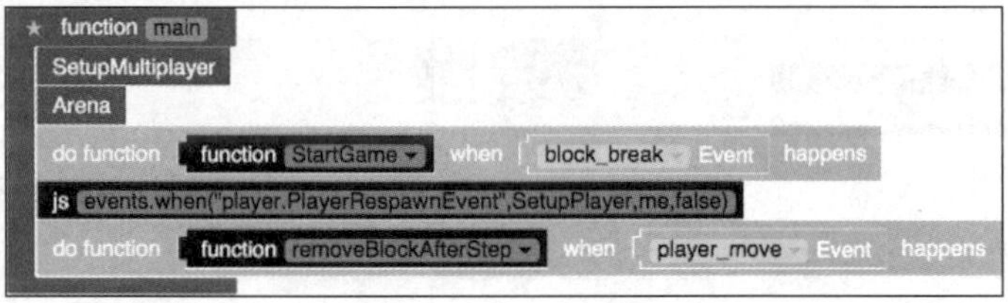

Figure 6-10

a. Since the first function call in main is SetupMultiplayer, look at that function.

SetupMultiplayer, shown in Figure 6-8, is the one I made for my multiplayer version, so nothing needs to change.

b. The second line in main is the call to the arena function. Figure 6-11 shows the arena function.

c. The arena function only builds the arena. It has no indication of players in the game, so nothing needs to change here, either.

d. The next line in main is the event that is triggered when a block is broken. When any player breaks a block, the StartGame function is called.

e. In your StartGame function, change the me block to a Player named Player1 block, as shown in the yellow box in Figure 6-12.

```
★ function Arena
   sarah-ArenaBuilder.init
   sarah-ArenaBuilder.ArenaWithFence
                         FenceHeight   | 1
                         PlatformSize  | 20
                         PlatformWidth | 1
                         ArenaMaterial | BRICK
                         FillMaterial  | LAVA
   sarah-ArenaBuilder.move_drone
                         direction     " up "
                         distance      | 2
   sarah-ArenaBuilder.ArenaWithFence
                         FenceHeight   | 5
                         PlatformSize  | 20
                         PlatformWidth | 1
                         ArenaMaterial | DIAMOND_BLOCK
                         FillMaterial  | AIR
   sarah-ArenaBuilder.SetArenaCenter
```

Figure 6-11

```
★ function StartGame with: info
   set block ▾ to   info ▾ 's block
   set block_type ▾ to  block ▾ 's type
   ★ if   block_type ▾  = ▾  MELON_BLOCK
   do   Teleport  Player named  Player1 ▾  to  sarah-ArenaBuilder.GetArenaCenter
        perform command  " gamemode s "  for player  Player named  Player1 ▾
        set blocksDestroyed ▾ to  0
```

Figure 6-12

f. The next line in main is the event that is triggered when a player respawns. When any player respawns, the Setup-Player function is called.

g. In the SetupPlayer function, replace the two me blocks with the Player named Player1 block, as shown in Figure 6-13.

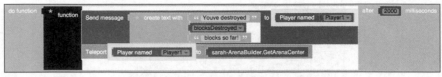

Figure 6-13

h. Add an `if` statement to ensure that the player who respawned was Player1 and not any other player in the Minecraft world (see Figure 6-14). This is in preparation for later in this project, when I show you how to add other players to your Minecraft world.

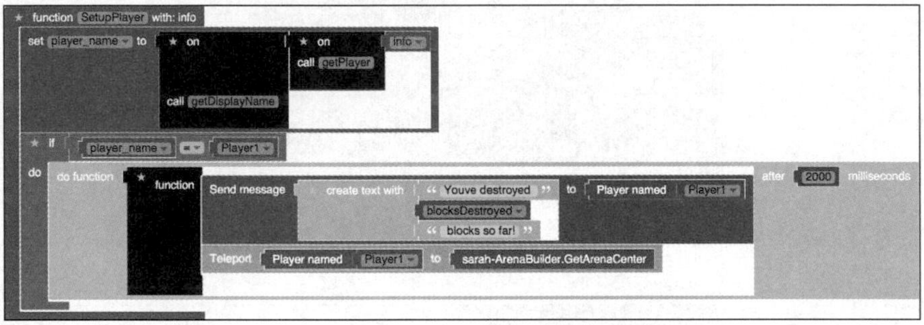

Figure 6-14

i. In the respawn event line in `main` (see Figure 6-15) is a reference to `me`. It doesn't have to be changed, because `me` is the player who launched the mod. Regardless of who is playing the multiplayer Spleef game, the game-launcher (`me`) is the only one who finds out whenever *anyone* respawns (this is also described as `me` *receiving the event*).

js events.when("player.PlayerRespawnEvent",SetupPlayer,me,false)

Figure 6-15

The final line in `main` is the event that is triggered when a player moves.

j. Change the final line so that Player1 (instead of me) triggers this event.

Figure 6-16 shows the change you make to main.

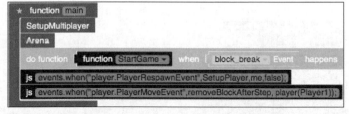

Figure 6-16

k. When any player moves, the function removeBlockAfter-Step is called.

Change the removeBlockAfterStep function to ensure that it was Player1 who moved, as shown in Figure 6-17.

First get the name of the player who moved, and then use an if statement to ensure that it was Player1.

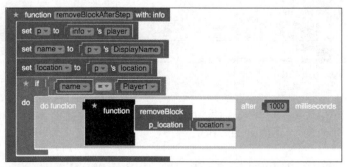

Figure 6-17

l. The removeBlockAfterStep function calls the remove-Block function. In this function, you're sending a message to me, but you want to send it to the player who just made a block disappear.

m. Add a parameter named p_name, and send the function the name of the player who just moved.

Figure 6-18 shows how to change removeBlock and removeBlockAfterStep.

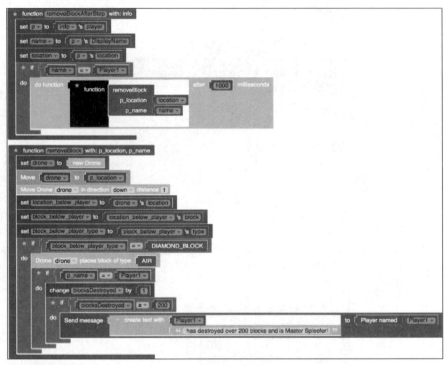

Figure 6-18

Figure 6-19 shows the entire code block you now have for your Spleef multiplayer mod.

Test your mod to make sure that it behaves exactly as the original Spleef game (described in Project 4) behaved. There should be no changes to how you play and what happens during play; it's still the single-player version of Spleef.

TIP

If you don't recall how the original single-player version of the Spleef game works, go back and experiment with it first, and then with the multiplayer version, to make sure that they both do the same thing.

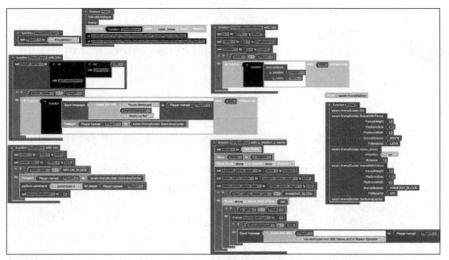

Figure 6-19

Iteration 2: Add in Player2

After Iteration 1 (making your Spleef game independent of the me block) you can move on to Iteration 2 and add in another player so that your game becomes multiplayer. In this section, I walk you through the exact same process as the section "Iteration 1: Refactor the Single-Player Version."

To add Player2, follow these steps:

1. Start with main and look at the first function, SetupMulti-player. Add another variable named Player2, and put the Minecraft username of the second player there.

   Figure 6-20 shows an example where the two players are thoughtstem and thoughtstem2.

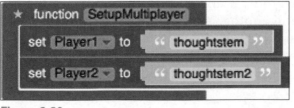

Figure 6-20

It's difficult to test the multiplayer version of Spleef without having a real-life second player to join you, so (in this section) work with a friend who also has Minecraft and who can join your server when you're ready to test.

Back in `main`, the next function is `arena`. The previous section explains that the `arena` function doesn't need to know what players are playing, so you can skip to the next line.

The third line in `main` is the event that calls the `StartGame` function when a block is broken.

2. In the `StartGame` function, make sure both players are set to Survival mode. Also, because you don't know which player broke the melon block, make sure both players are teleported to the center of the arena.

   Figure 6-21 shows how to make those changes.

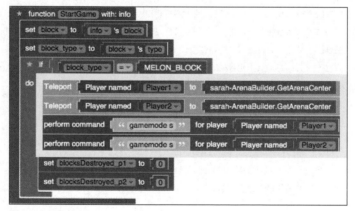

Figure 6-21

3. Still in the `StartGame` function, rename the `blocks Destroyed` variable to become more specific to Player1, and then add another variable for blocks destroyed for Player2, as shown in Figure 6-22.

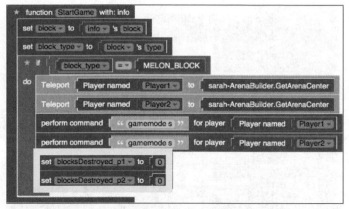

Figure 6-22

4. Back in main, the next line is the event that is called whenever a player respawns.

   a. The SetupPlayer is called. To make SetupPlayer multiplayer-safe, add an else-if statement to the if statement that essentially does the same as Player1, but for Player2.

   b. Add a second message to let each player know how many blocks the other player has broken.

   Figure 6-23 shows all these changes to the SetupPlayer function.

   Be sure to use all the right variables for Player1 and Player2 or else when Player1 respawns, it will teleport Player2 back to the arena.

5. Back in main, the next line is the event that is called when a player moves; the removeBlockAfterStep function is called. Figure 6-24 shows the change to the if statement that takes place. If either Player1 or Player2 was the one who moved, call the removeBlock function.

6. Change the removeBlock function also, to increment the correct blocksDestroyed counter and to announce the name of the 200-block destroyer.

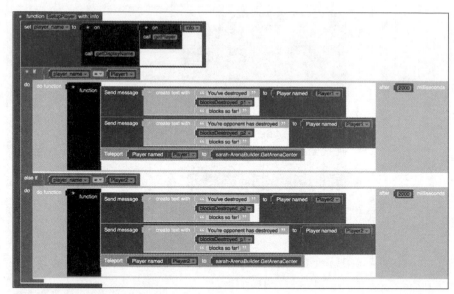

Figure 6-23

Figure 6-24

Figure 6-25 shows how to change this `if` statement. (***Note:*** The fireworks display has been removed.)

You're done! Figures 6-26 and 6-27 show the final batches of code, which you can also see at

```
mod.learntomod.com/programs/sarah-Spleef_Multi
    player
```

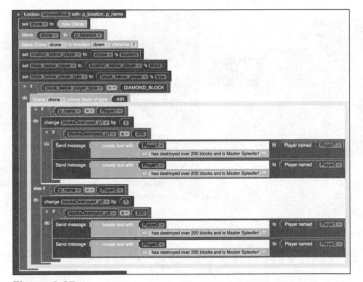

Figure 6-25

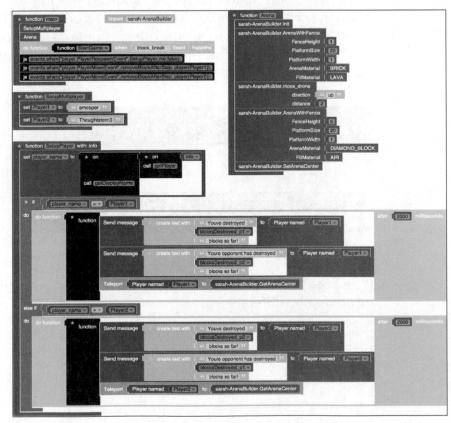

Figure 6-26

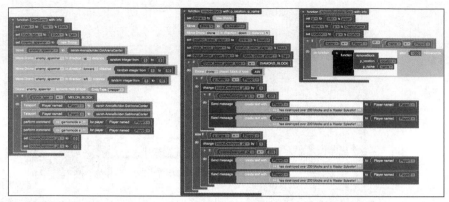

Figure 6-27

Test the Multiplayer Spleef Game

To test this multiplayer version of Spleef, launch Minecraft and go to the LearnToMod server as I showed you in Project 1. Then type the command /open, as shown in Figure 6-28. This opens your Minecraft world to anyone else who has access to the LearnToMod server, but the only way they can get in is if they know the number that you see in Figure 6-29.

Figure 6-28

Figure 6-29

You see the message shown in Figure 6-29, but your number will probably be different.

Have a friend first join the LearnToMod server and then type the command **/join ##**, where ## represents the number displayed in your server when you type the open command. For example, Figure 6-30 shows what the other person would type if the message is the one shown in Figure 6-29.

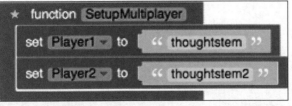

Figure 6-30

Make sure the Minecraft usernames that are in your Setup-Mulitplayer function are those of you and your friends. For example, if your Minecraft username is thoughtstem and your friend's username is thoughtstem2, your SetupMultiplayer function would look like Figure 6-31.

Figure 6-31

Click Mod in your LearnToMod account, and then run the Spleef_Multiplayer mod in Minecraft. You and your friend are teleported to the center of the arena, as shown in Figure 6-32.

When one of you breaks the melon block, you both should start making blocks below you disappear, as shown in Figure 6-33.

Play the multiplayer version to make sure you have written all of the code correctly as you think it should be.

Figure 6-32

Figure 6-33

Iteration 3: End the Game at 200 Blocks

You should have the multiplayer version of Spleef end whenever one player reaches 200 blocks. Before doing this, however, revisit your scene. Only 400 blocks are on the platform, so it might be difficult to achieve the goal of destroying 200 blocks because it would mean that a player would have to destroy exactly half of the blocks to win, minimizing the number of strategies (like destroying blocks on opposite sides of the arena) that the players can use. An easy fix is to double the size of the arena.

Here's a quick fix: In the `Arena` function, change `PlatformSize` from 20 to 40 for both the lava platform and the diamond arena, as shown in Figure 6-34.

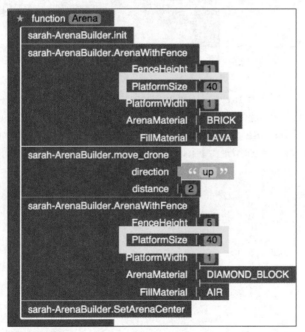

Figure 6-34

Now, in the `removeBlock` function, an easy way to end the game is to set both players to Creative mode, and move them to the arena's center (which is directly above the arena). Figure 6-35 shows the three changes you need to make to end the game when one player destroys 200 blocks: in the `removeBlock`, `StartGame`, and `endGame` functions.

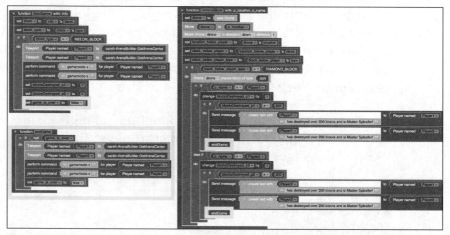

Figure 6-35

Congratulations! You have successfully made a multiplayer version of Spleef! Be sure to continue building onto this game (maybe try adding a third player), test out all of the changes you make in Iteration 3, and remember: Have fun!

Part 3
Designing and Building a Multiplayer Minigame

```
★ function  on_land  with: info
  ★  if  |  sarah-Projectile_Library.check_if_launched
  do    Send message   " Now Exploding! "   to   player ▾
        create explosion that  destroys ▾  blocks  sets ▾  fire to blocks  at location   location of   info ▾  's  block
        sarah-Projectile_Library.destroy
                        block   info ▾  's  block
```

This week you'll build:

Modding with Projectiles

Being able to build objects, send drones out, or trigger events can be fun; but being able to cast mods out into the world and have them affect the area around where they land is *powerful*. In this project, I show you how to make and run a mod that projects a block into the world and causes an explosion when it lands.

Design and Build an Exploding Projectile

In this section, I show you how to write a mod that, when run in Minecraft, causes a block to be thrown from your location. When the block lands, it causes an explosion, destroying anything around it. You can later modify this fun, powerful mod to have it do other things also, such as teleport you to where it landed.

Design the launch and explosion

Before you start coding, plan your strategy. Writing this exploding projectile mod isn't as complex as a minigame mod, but you need to design its complex pieces still (such as where it should be thrown from and what should happen when it lands).

For starters, you have to define these two actions to make the block

🖛 Launch when the mod is run

🖛 Explode when it lands

Plan the block launch

When you run your mod, make a block (maybe bedrock) to start from your position and move up and away from you. Designing the code for a three-dimensional (3D) mod is kind of tricky because you can't draw it easily on paper. (3D involves six directions: up, down, left, right, *forward,* and *backward*). To write this 3D mod, you use *x*-, *y*-, and *z*-coordinates to plan out where the block will start and how it will move. Check out the following Math Connections paragraph for an explanation of *x*-, *y*-, and *z*- coordinates, if you don't already know about them.

When you draw something on paper, you're making a 2D drawing. You know that something is 2D because it has only four directions (up, down, left, and right). In math, up and down are represented by the y-axis (a higher value for y is up and a lower value for y is down). Left and right are represented by the x-axis (a higher value for x is right, and a lower value for y is left). This makes *x*-coordinate and *y*-coordinate easy to see in 2D space.

Figure 7-1 shows a 2D *x-y* plane with a dot at the position *x*=1 and *y*=3, which can also be represented as (1,3).

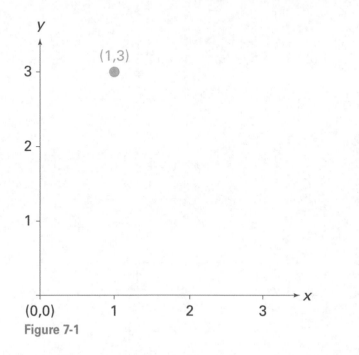

Figure 7-1

To understand the 3D world, you have to introduce another direction (forward and backward), and in math, this is represented by a third coordinate: z. Figure 7-2 shows a third line that represents the *z*-plane moving into the screen. The green dot is the same dot from Figure 7-1; it's at (1,3,0). The red dot is at (1, 3, 4) and is actually deep into the screen.

Figure 7-3 shows how a cube would look on the *x-, y-, z-* planes. The green dot from Figure 7-2 would be on the blue side, flat up against the screen, and the red dot would be along the red side, deep into the screen.

One way to make the block launch is to teleport (move) the block to a specific location using the teleport block in LearnToMod. You can teleport the block to (1,1,1) then (2,2,2) then (3,3,3) then (4,4,4) and so on. This *could* work, but if you search through your LearnToMod blocks, you will find some useful blocks in the Minecraft⇨Block category, as you can see in Figure 7-4.

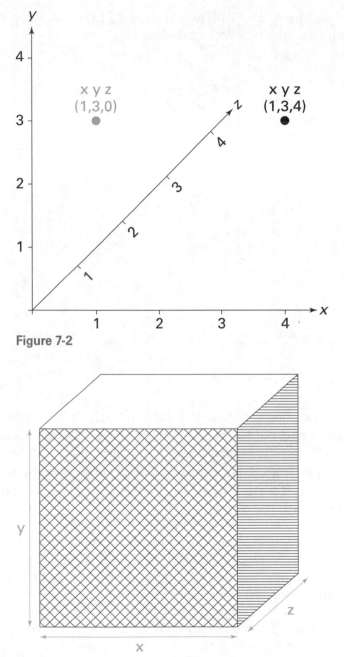

Figure 7-2

Figure 7-3

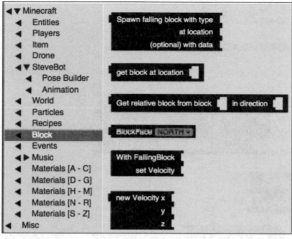

Figure 7-4

A *falling block* can be launched, and it falls as it moves through space, just as though you were to throw a ball in the real world: It would go up into the air first, and then it would fall in a 3D space (the real world).

Even without writing the code yet, you can plan out the final code by dragging blocks into the programming environment that you're likely to use, as shown in Figure 7-5.

Plan the block explosion

Once you launch your block, as described in the preceding section, you should make it explode when it hits the ground. You can review the LearnToMod blocks to find the create explosion block under the Minecraft⇨World category, as shown in Figure 7-6, which you can use to make the block explode when it hits the ground.

Similarly to my instruction in the previous section, you can plan out the explode function as shown in Figure 7-7.

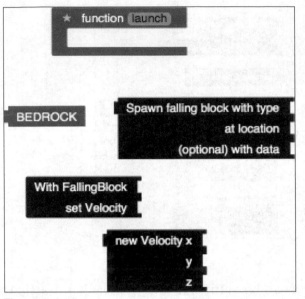

Figure 7-5

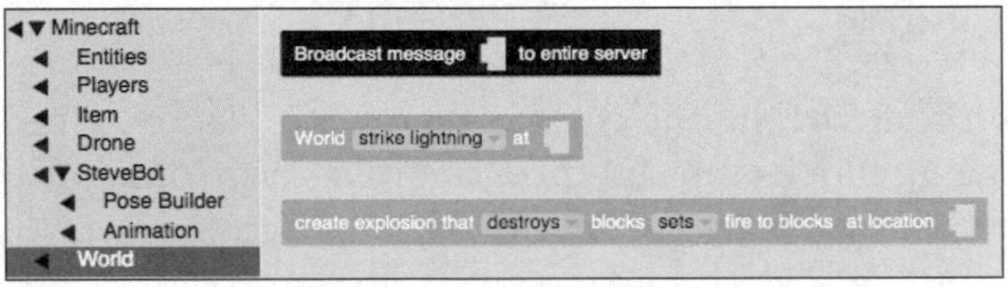

Figure 7-6

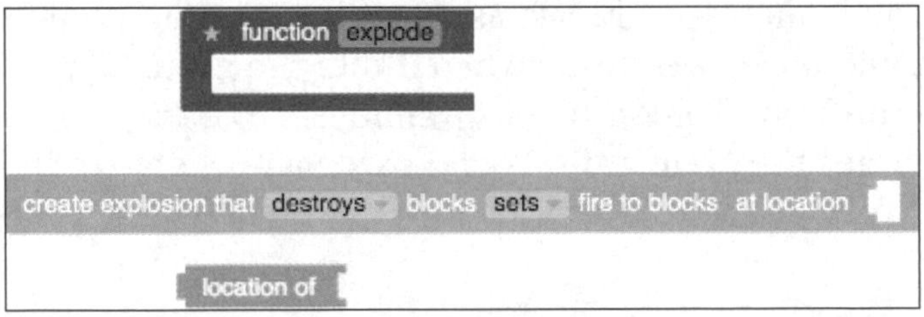

Figure 7-7

Keep track of state

An important aspect to keep track of in the exploding projectile mod is the state of the block. *State* describes what the block is doing at this moment. To see an example, you can track your own state for an entire day, and you can use a *state-machine* (a diagram that tracks data about the events in the world) to keep track of it, as shown in Figure 7-8.

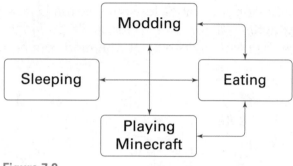

Figure 7-8

In this mod, state is important to keep track of because you don't want the block to explode before you launched it, or before it lands. If it explodes too soon, it won't destroy your target (the place where it lands). State-machines are useful representations of all possible states in the world (or at least all the ones you care about). Figure 7-8 shows you how to make a state-machine about your real life, as it applies to playing Minecraft.

As you can see in Figure 7-8, you might be in one of these four states (in real-life):

✔ Asleep

✔ Eating

✔ Modding

✔ Playing Minecraft

If you follow the direction of the arrow from the Asleep state shown in the figure, you can see that the only action you can take when you leave that state — or when you wake up — is to eat (probably breakfast). By following the directions of the arrows again, you can see that after you eat, you can either mod or play Minecraft. You can rotate between eating, modding, and playing Minecraft all you want. But if you want to go to sleep again, you have to eat first (probably dinner).

The state-machine for your block looks something like Figure 7-9. The lines show actions that *must* happen if the previous one happens, and once the block is destroyed, the mod is over and you can run it again.

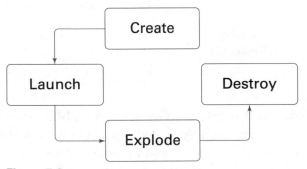

Figure 7-9

The state-machine in Figure 7-9 is simpler than your Minecraft day state-machine in Figure 7-8 because your block can take only one path through it. Once it is created, it *must* be launched, then it *must* explode, then it *must* be destroyed. Once it has been destroyed, the mod is completed.

Running the mod initiates the create state, but it is useful to keep track of whether the block has been launched and whether it has been exploded. Figure 7-10 shows the two variables you should add to keep track of the state of the block.

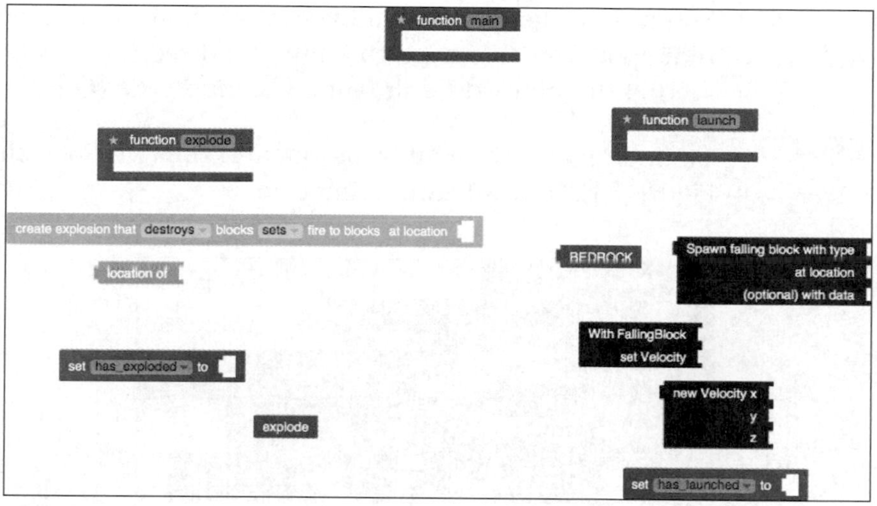

Figure 7-10

Iteration 1: Set up the launch event

Even though this mod has no gameplay loop (as you do in Projects 4, 5, and 6), you should still write this mod iteratively. In the first iteration, you make the block launch when you run the mod. Follow these steps:

1. Send a message when you enter the launch function to make sure that when you run your mod, the launch function gets called.

   Figure 7-11 shows the code example.

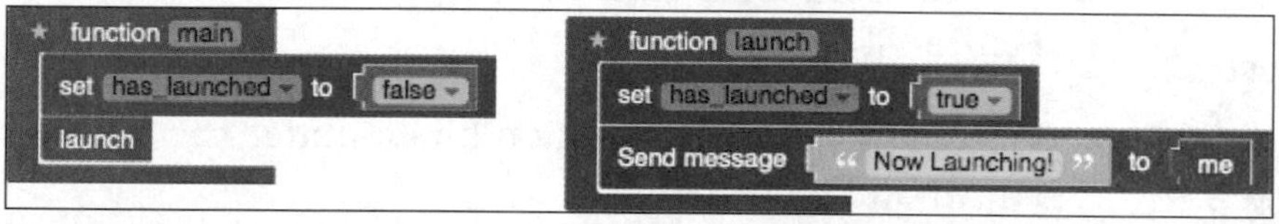

Figure 7-11

2. You need to get your location so that the block launches from that spot. You also need to know the direction you are facing so that the block doesn't launch behind you. (Ouch!)

To find this location information, add the two lines shown in Figure 7-12 to the launch function.

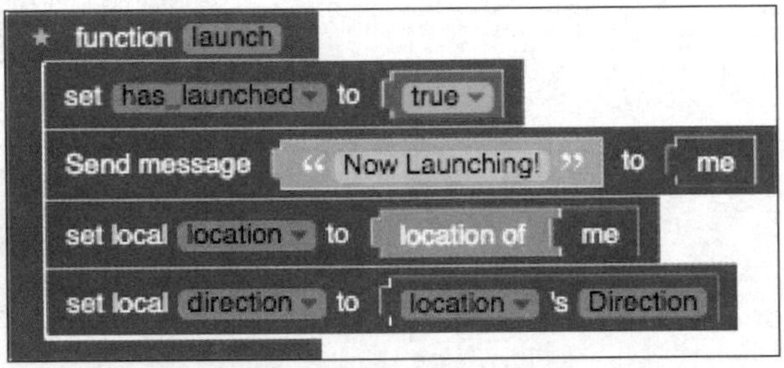

Figure 7-12

Local variables are visible only to the function they're in — and this step uses local variables instead of regular variables. If you make the local variable location in the launch function, main and explode won't even know that location variable exists. Local variables are useful when you're creating a large mod, because then you can have a local location variable in five different functions. Each function will be able to see only its specific location variable, so if you change the value in one function, the other functions don't accidentally use that new value. They don't even know it exists.

3. You can find local variables in the Misc category, as shown in Figure 7-13.

4. Find the location's Direction block under the Misc category, as shown in Figure 7-14.

5. Now you can use the FallingBlock blocks shown earlier, in Figure 7-5.

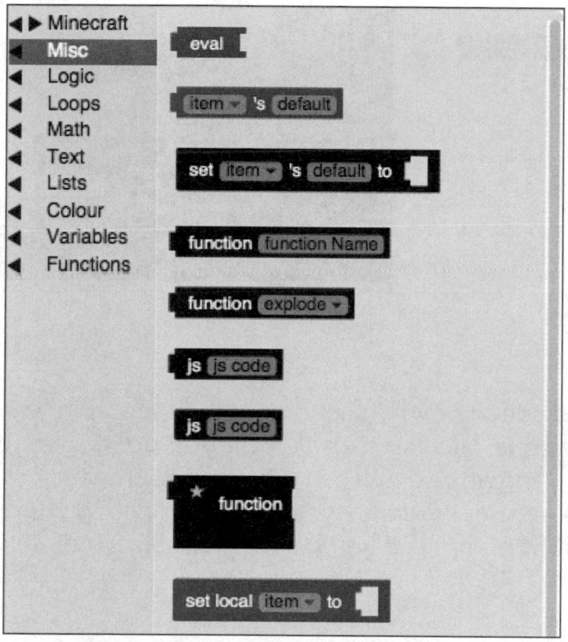

Figure 7-13

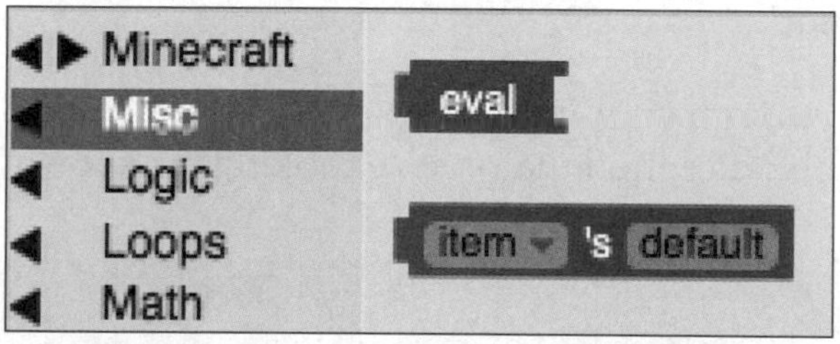

Figure 7-14

To spawn (create) a falling block of type Bedrock at your location, set the block's velocity to double what it was by multiplying it by 2. By doubling the velocity, the block starts moving away from you (refer to Figure 7-3).

Figure 7-15 shows you how to set it up.

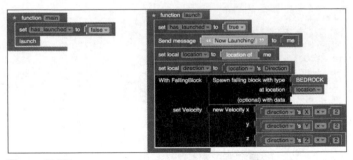

Figure 7-15

MATH CONNECTIONS
1
+1
2

Velocity is the speed of an object plus the direction in which it is moving. Speed is calculated as how far you go in a certain amount of time, such as moving 20 miles in 1 hour. That means you're moving at "20 miles per hour." Velocity is the difference in your position in a certain amount of time, so you'll also know which direction the object is moving.

6. After you've ensured that the only blocks you have are the ones shown in Figure 7-15 (all others should be disabled), test your mod.

When you run your mod, you see a bedrock block thrown from you in the direction that you're looking, as shown in Figure 7-16.

Figure 7-16

Iteration 2: Set up the explode event

After you're sure that your block can launch, you need to register when it lands, because that's when it should explode. To set up the `explode` event, follow these steps:

1. Revisit the state-machine shown earlier, in Figure 7-9.

   Your block should explode only *if* you have already launched it. When it's exploding, it's no longer launching. Figure 7-17 shows how the `explode` function updates the state of your mod using the launching and exploding variables.

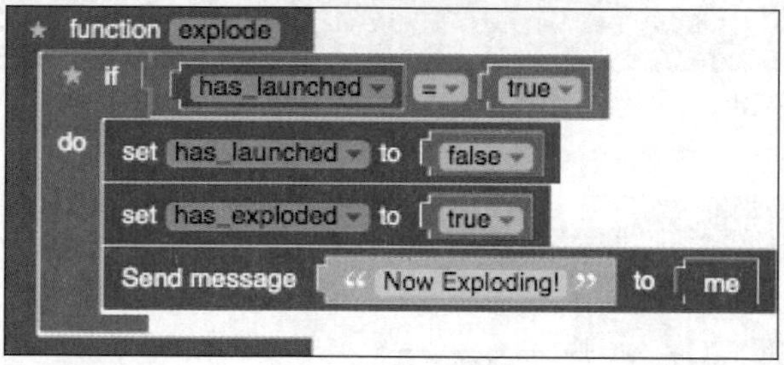

   Figure 7-17

2. Test the mod.

   You see a scene like the one shown in Figure 7-18. When the block hits something, you see the message `Now Exploding!`.

3. Add the `info` parameter to the `explode` function and use it to get information about the block that triggered the event.

   Because this function is being called from an event, a certain block (the bedrock block that you launched) triggers the event. You can use the info parameter to get the location where the bedrock landed and cause an explosion around that location. Then set the exploding variable to `false`, because it is no longer exploding. Figure 7-19 shows the code for these changes.

4. Test your code.

   You see a scene like the one shown in Figure 7-20, where an explosion takes place on the spot where the bedrock block lands.

Now Launching!
Now Exploding!

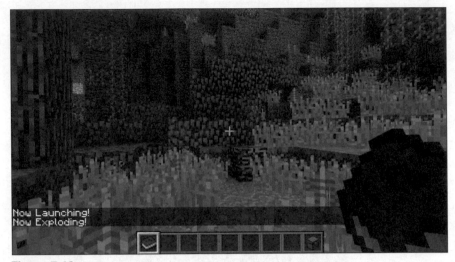

Figure 7-18

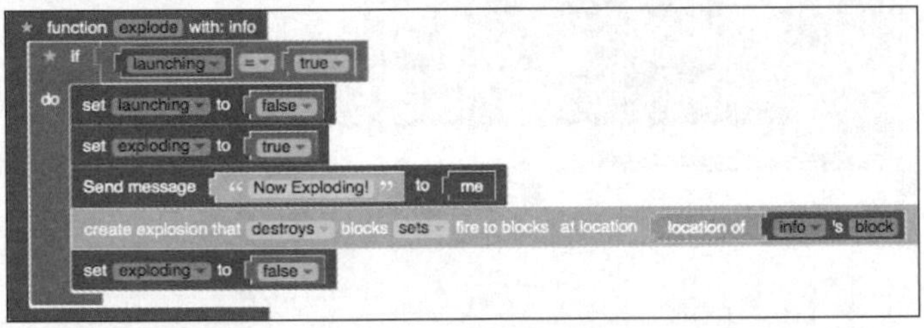

function explode with: info
if launching = true
do
set launching to false
set exploding to true
Send message " Now Exploding! " to me
create explosion that destroys blocks sets fire to blocks at location location of info 's block
set exploding to false

Figure 7-19

Commands Run
smesper
Now Launching!
Now Exploding!

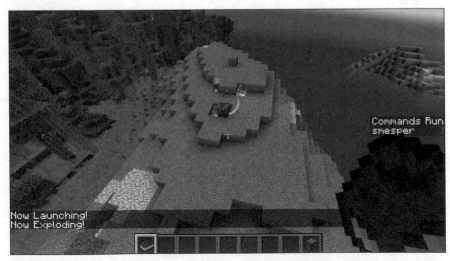

Figure 7-20

Iteration 3: Set up the destroy event

You may have noticed that the bedrock block isn't destroyed during the explosion. To do make it disappear (to destroy it), you can use a technique that I use in the Spleef minigame (described in Project 4) — replace the block with air! Figure 7-21 shows you how to do it.

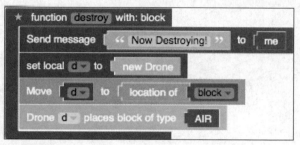

Figure 7-21

To start, call the `destroy` function from the `explode` function, as shown in Figure 7-22.

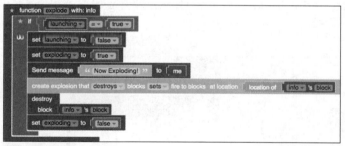

Figure 7-22

When you test the mod, you see an explosion, and the bedrock block disappears, as shown in Figure 7-23.

Iteration 4: Refactor and check the state-machine

Even though you have now finished writing the code for this mod, mods aren't complete unless they're easy to use. In this section,

I tell you how to complete Iteration 4, where you refactor your code to make it cleaner and easier to understand.

Figure 7-23

Figure 7-24 shows all the code that you have written in this project, and it looks just like the drawing of the state-machine in Figure 7-25.

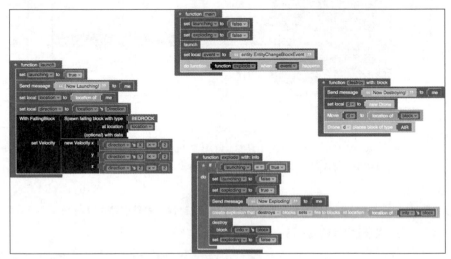

Figure 7-24

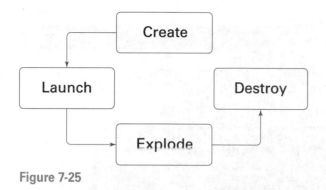

Figure 7-25

To make sure that you're transitioning into states correctly (going from one state to another), look at your code and make sure it matches these steps:

1. Change the main function to match the one shown in Figure 7-26.

   When you run your mod, the main function is called. The main function calls the launch function, and sets up the event to trigger the explode function when the block hits something.

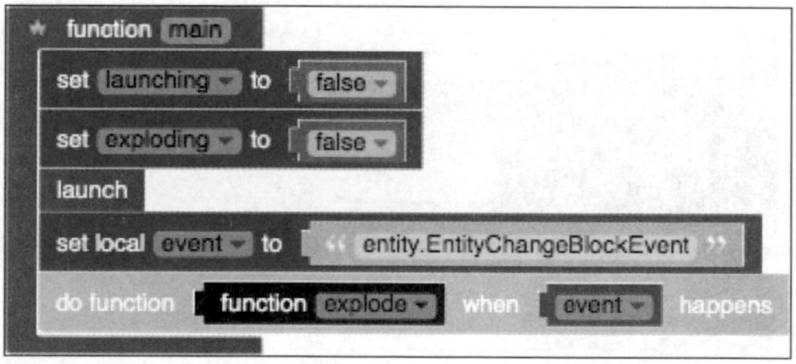

   ```
   function main
     set launching to    false
     set exploding to    false
     launch
     set local event to    "  entity.EntityChangeBlockEvent  "
     do function    function explode    when    event    happens
   ```

Figure 7-26

2. Change the launch function to match Figure 7-27.

   The main function calls the launch function, which happens only if the projectile isn't already launching or exploding.

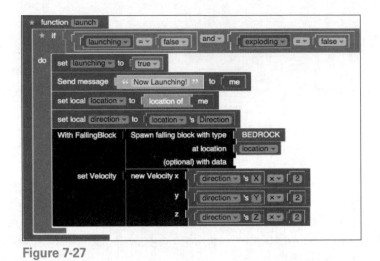

Figure 7-27

3. Change the `explode` function to match Figure 7-28.

The `explode` function is called whenever the `main` function notices that the block has hit something (because it has the event that simply waits for a block to hit something). It's called only if the block was being launched and it isn't already exploding.

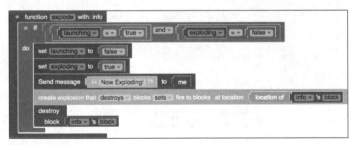

Figure 7-28

4. Change the `destroy` function to match Figure 7-29.

The `destroy` function is called when the `explode` function finishes blowing everything up, but it happens only if the block is no longer launching — and is actually exploding.

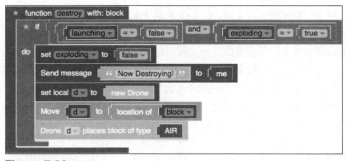

Figure 7-29

By the end of exploding projectile, both the launching and exploding variables need to be set to `false` again. The entire code example looks like the one shown in Figure 7-30.

Congratulations — you have made an exploding projectile!

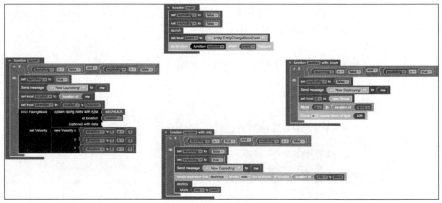

Figure 7-30

When you test your code, it should do the same thing as in the previous section.

When code is *refactored,* the code changes but its effects do not.

Make a Projectile Library

You can make lots of projectile effects in addition to exploding. Rather than rebuild all the projectile code from scratch, you can *abstract* the projectile state-machine (make it a projectile state-machine for any effect, not just exploding) and create a library that helps you build a lot of different projectiles.

A *library* is a mod that lets you call functions from other mods. In Project 4, I show you how to use the ArenaBuilder library to call the `arena` function to build an arena.

Set up the projectile mods

To set up the projectile mod, copy the projectile mod that I explain how to make in the preceding section. Follow these steps:

1. Click the Actions tab and then choose the Copy command, as shown in Figure 7-31.

   You see two versions of the projectile mod, as shown in Figure 7-32.

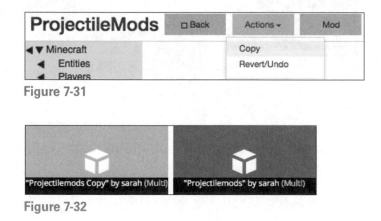

Figure 7-31

Figure 7-32

2. Open one mod and rename it Projectile_Library, as shown in Figure 7-33.

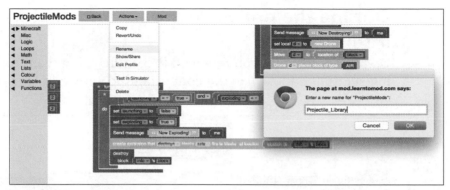

Figure 7-33

3. Open the other mod and rename it `Exploding_Projectile`, as shown in Figure 7-34.

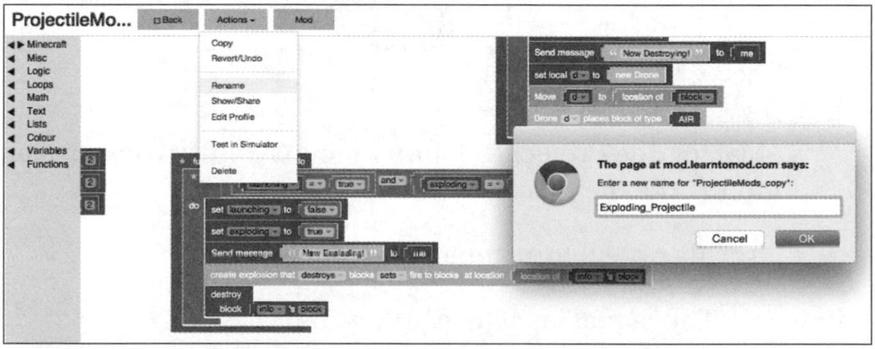

Figure 7-34

The two mods renamed mods are shown in Figure 7-35.

Figure 7-35

Outline the projectile library and explosion projectile mods

Open the mod that you renamed Projectile_Library in the preceding section. It looks like the code example shown in Figure 7-36.

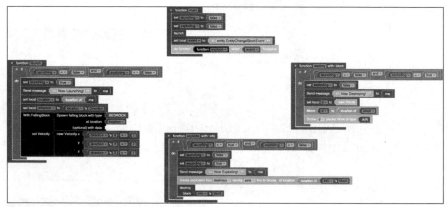

Figure 7-36

Making the Projectile_Library mod is a little tricky because it has to handle the following information:

✔ All state information, like launching

✔ The actual launching

✔ Destruction of the projectile

But the Explosion_Projectile mod needs to handle

✔ The type of block to launch

✔ The actions that should happen when the block lands

In the next two sections, I walk you through the steps to change the Projectile_Library mod and the Explosion_Projectile mod.

Make one more copy of your mod and name it Original_Explosion_ Projectile, just in case you mess up and need to get back to a working mod.

Change the main and launch functions

The first list in the previous section specifies the information that the Projectile_Library should handle. In this section, however, I tell you how to actually make the changes in your code.

To make changes to the `main` function, follow these steps:

1. Rename the `main` function `init`.

   Because this mod is now a library, the functions in it are called from other mods — though the library itself isn't run in Minecraft.

2. *Export* this function (make it accessible from other mods) so that it can be accessed from the Explosion_Projectile mod. Figure 7-37 shows how the function should look. You can find the export block under the Misc category, as you can see in Figure 7-38.

```
export  init

★  function  init  with: launch_block

   set  launching ▾  to   false ▾

   set  exploding ▾  to   false ▾

   launch

   set local  event ▾  to   “ entity.EntityChangeBlockEvent ”

   do function   function  explode ▾   when   event ▾   happens
```

Figure 7-37

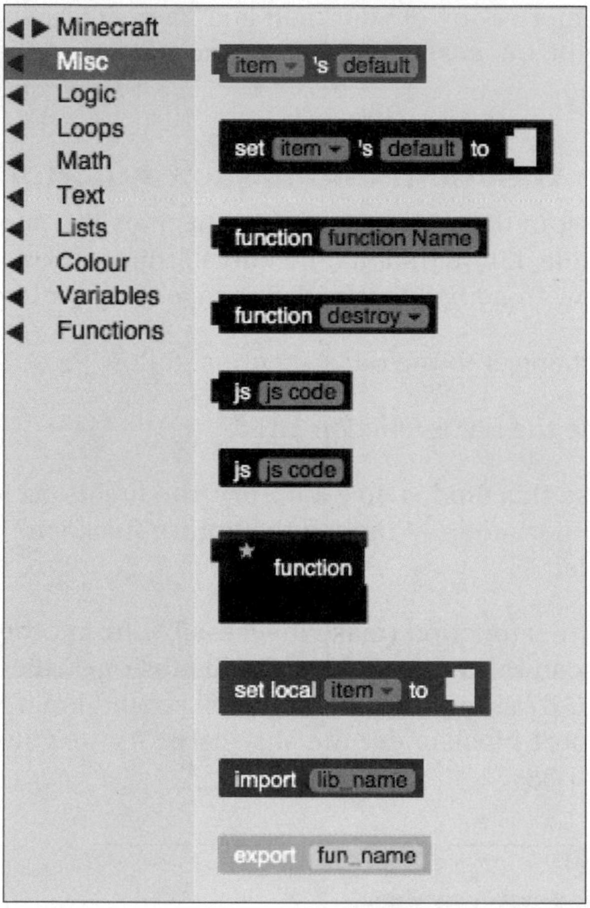

Figure 7-38

3. Add a parameter named `launch_block` to the `init` function that defines the type of block to be launched, and save the parameter in a variable named `block_type`.

   Figure 7-39 shows the changes you make.

4. Delete the event.

   This step is handled by the `Exploding_Projectile` mod. The library doesn't handle it, because you may want other things to trigger the effects later on. Figure 7-40 shows the changes to make.

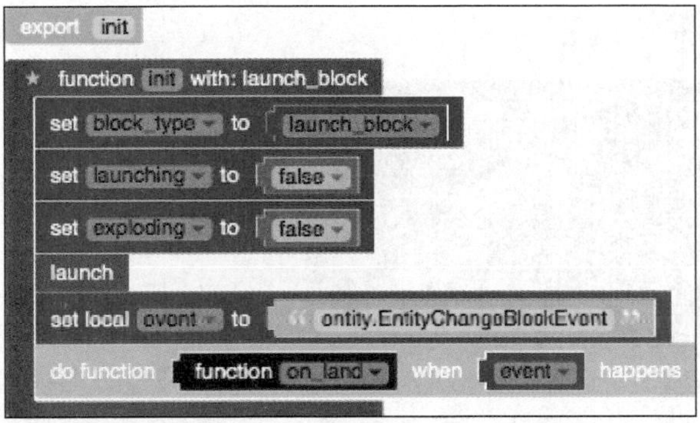

Figure 7-39

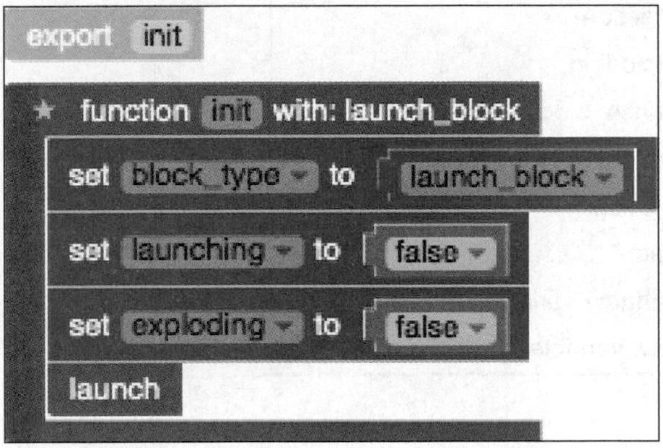

Figure 7-40

5. To name the exploding variable landing, click the drop-down arrow next to the word *exploding* and choose Rename Variable from the menu, as shown in Figure 7-41.

Renaming the variable is shown in Figure 7-42.

Your init should look like the one shown in Figure 7-43.

After you complete this step list, you may want to make a minor change to the launch function. Figure 7-44 shows how to change the bedrock block to the block_type variable instead; that way, the type of block is decided in the Explosion_Projectile mod.

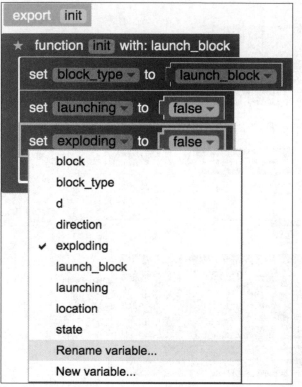

Figure 7-41

Figure 7-42

The landing variable updates by itself when you rename it, as shown in Figure 7-43.

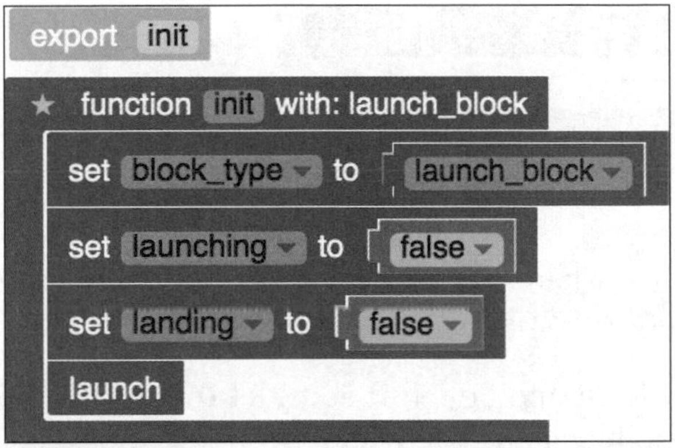

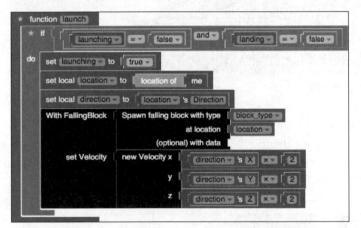

Figure 7-43

Figure 7-44

Change the explode function

To make changes to the `explode` function, you first need to change it to a function that has a return value. The purpose of this function, in the library, is to let the other mod know whether the block has already been launched. Follow these steps:

1. Rename the function to `check_if_launched`.

   Figure 7-45 shows the new function block you have.

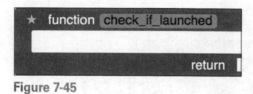

Figure 7-45

2. Make a new variable named `launched` and initialize (give it the value) it to `false`, as shown in Figure 7-46.

   This variable should be returned to let the other mod know whether the block has been launched.

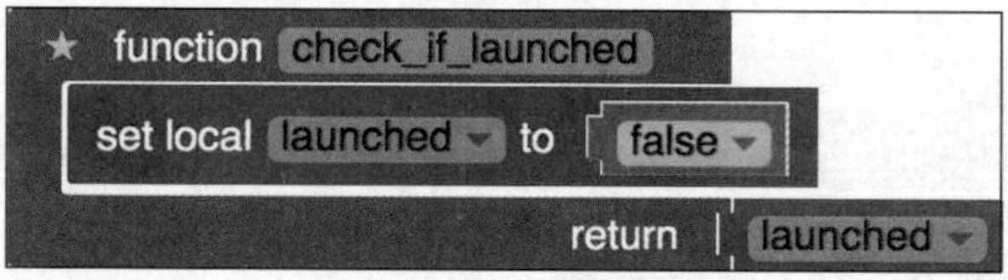

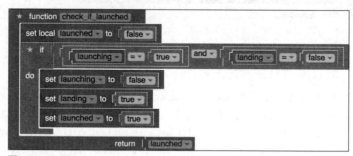

Figure 7-46

3. You need the `if` statement from the original `explode` function, but instead of sending a message and exploding and destroying anything around the block, just set the launched variable to `true`, as shown in Figure 7-47.

Figure 7-47

4. Export this function too so that the other mod can check to see whether the block has been launched.

   Figure 7-48 shows you how.

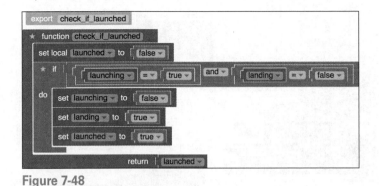

Figure 7-48

Change the destroy function

You also need to update the destroy function to look like the example shown in Figure 7-49. Follow these steps:

1. Add a parameter named block, which is the block that needs to be destroyed.

2. Change the info's block to the parameter block.

3. Export the destroy function.

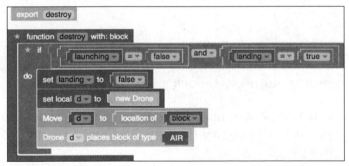

Figure 7-49

Congratulations! You have completed the Projectile_Library mod. The entire mod should look like the one shown in Figure 7-50.

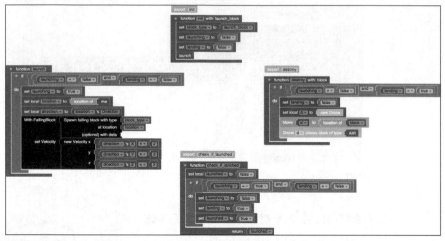

Figure 7-50

Change the Explosion_Projectile mod

After the library is written, you can define what happens in the Explosion_Projectile mod. First, open the Explosion_Projectile mod and import the Projectile_Library that I tell you how to make in the preceding section. Then follow these steps:

1. Grab an import block from the Misc category, as shown in Figure 7-51.

2. Type your LearnToMod nickname and then **-Projectile_Library**. For example, if your LearnToMod nickname was *sarah*, your import block should look like Figure 7-52.

   Now you should make changes to the main function because you have the library that you just created and you need to call those new functions.

3. Remove everything from the main function, and delete all of the blocks except the event blocks. The two event blocks should go into a new function named on_land_event, but the function that should be called is a new function named on_land that has a parameter named info, as shown in Figure 7-53.

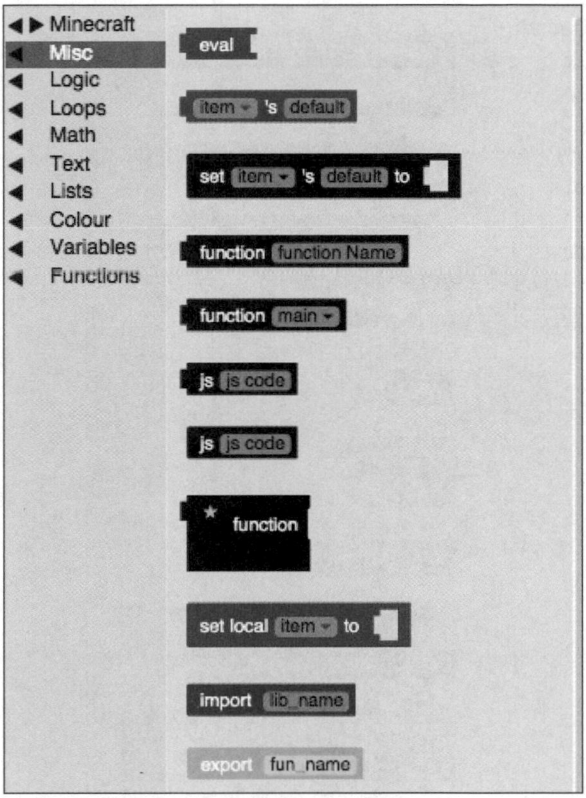

Figure 7-51

Figure 7-52

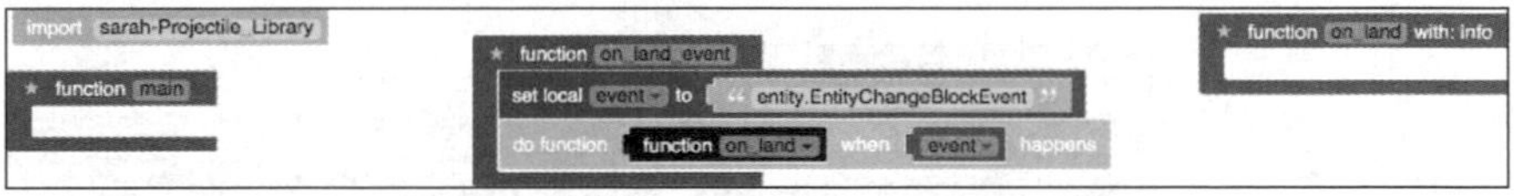

Figure 7-53

4. Look in the Functions category and you should see three new functions from the library you just made, as shown in Figure 7-54.

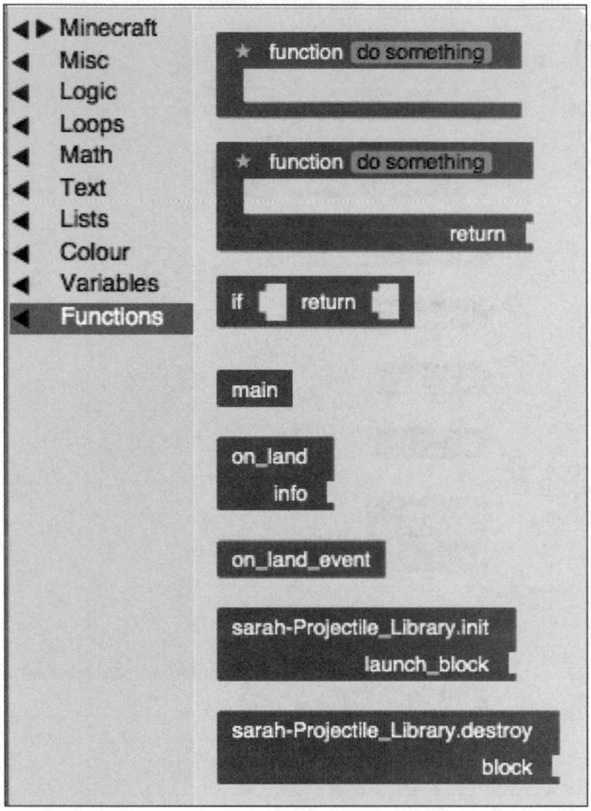

Figure 7-54

5. Add a call to the `Projectile_Library.init` function, with a parameter of Bedrock, and a call to the `on_land_event` function, as shown in Figure 7-55.

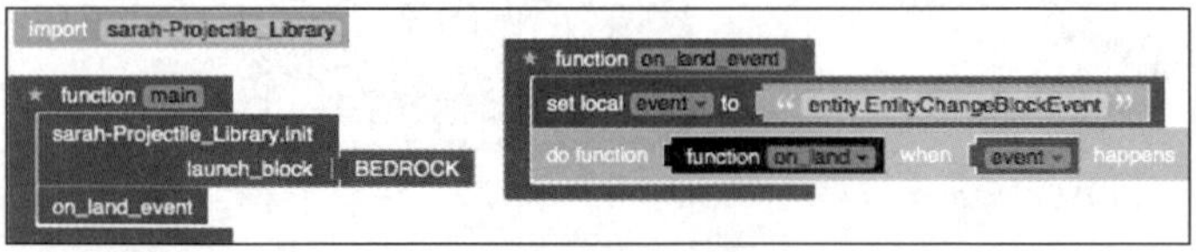

Figure 7-55

Finally, after you have fixed the `main` function, fill in the `on_land` function. Follow these steps:

1. Add an if-statement that calls the `Projectile_Library.` `check_if_launched` function, as shown in Figure 7-56.

Figure 7-56

2. Put the explosion code from the old `explode` function into the if-statement, as shown in Figure 7-57.

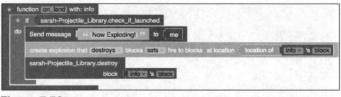

Figure 7-57

3. Make a call to the `Projectile_Library.destroy` function, as shown in Figure 7-58.

Figure 7-58

Congratulations! You have completed the code for the Explosion_ Projectile mod! Everything else in the mod can be deleted, so your entire mod should look like Figure 7-59.

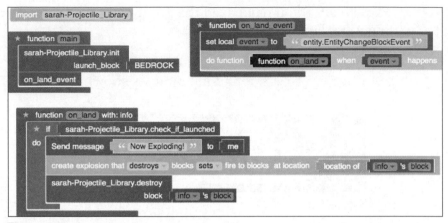

Figure 7-59

Test your new library

If you've followed along with all the steps in this project, you should now have two mods:

- **Projectile_Library:** It looks like the example shown earlier, in Figure 7-50.

- **Explosion_Projectile:** It looks like the example shown in Figure 7-59. When you test the Explosion_Projectile mod, you see a scene like the one shown in Figure 7-60.

Figure 7-60

Congratulations! You have successfully created a projectile library and used it to make an exploding projectile.

Complete an Extra Challenge: Use the Projectile Library to Make a Teleporting Projectile

Figure out a way to use your new projectile library to make a teleporting projectile. The projectile should teleport you to the block when it lands.

You need to change only the two blocks shown in Figure 7-61.

Figure 7-61

Making a Multiplayer Minigame: Capture the Flag

In Project 7, I show you how to create a Projectile library, which you can use to create a mod that causes an explosion and to create a mod that teleports you to another location.
I like to call these mods magic wands because, with only one motion, you can create a big effect! In this project, I explain how to create a Capture the Flag game where you use these wands to defend your flags, while you seek out your opponent's flags.

In the early 1980s, Scholastic released a Capture the Flag–style game on one of the first home computers. Since then, many games have used this as a reference for their games (Call of Duty, Halo, and Team Fortress 2 are just a few) because of the competition that Capture the Flag inspires. In this project, I show you how to turn Minecraft into a Capture the Flag game and how to craft the competition however you like!

Plan the Capture-the-Flag Game

Before you start coding, you should plan your two-player Capture the Flag game on paper. To plan, think about the game in layers. Layer 1 is where you set up the game for Capture the Flag. Layer 2 is where you set up your libraries to use during Capture the Flag. Figure 8-1 shows what happens at each layer, and the rest of this project walks you through the steps to build the Capture the Flag minigame mod.

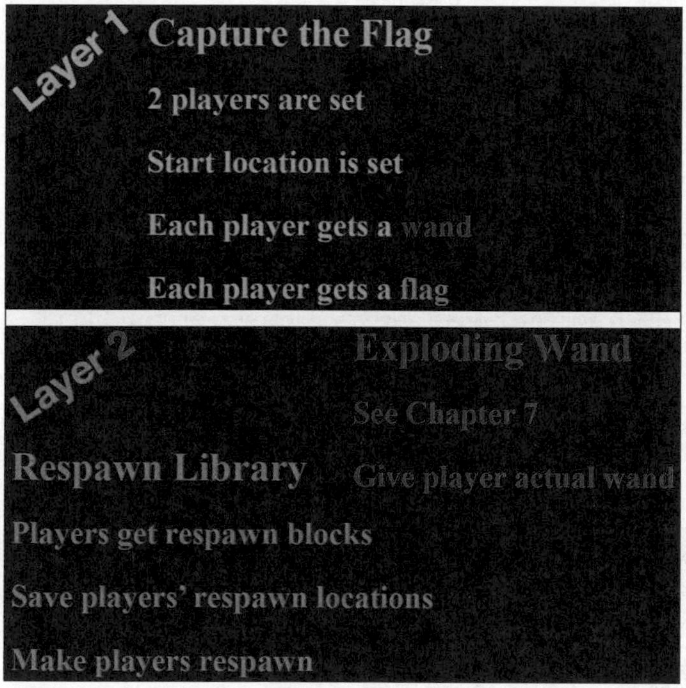

Capture the Flag

2 players are set

Start location is set

Each player gets a wand

Each player gets a flag

Exploding Wand

See Chapter 7

Respawn Library   Give player actual wand

Players get respawn blocks

Save players' respawn locations

Make players respawn

Figure 8-1

Prepare the Capture-the-Flag Mod

First, prepare the Capture the Flag mod on Layer 1:

1. Select Mod from the menu at the top of the homepage.

2. Create a new mod named `CaptureTheFlag`, as shown in Figure 8-2.

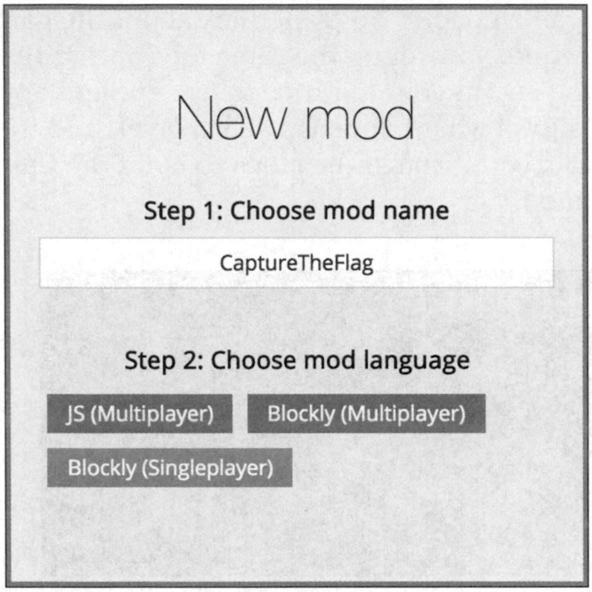

New mod

Step 1: Choose mod name

CaptureTheFlag

Step 2: Choose mod language

JS (Multiplayer)   Blockly (Multiplayer)

Blockly (Singleplayer)

Figure 8-2

3. Click the arrow (as shown in Figure 8-3) to enter the newly created mod, as shown in Figure 8-3.

See Inside
CaptureTheFlag by sarah

Figure 8-3

4. Click the Code box, as shown in Figure 8-4.

Now outline the mod that you want to create. Start out with a single player so that you can test the mod on your own.

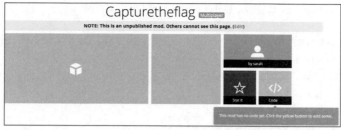

Figure 8-4

Make the gameplay loop

Imagine a gameplay loop for this iteration of the Capture the Flag mod. Figure 8-5 shows a simple gameplay loop with four iterations:

✔ **Start:** Make 1 player with 1 flag and 1 wand. A player who dies should respawn at their flag.

✔ **Challenge:** Add a second player with the same capabilities as Player 1.

Figure 8-5

✔ **Goal:** The goal is to destroy the other person's flag.

✔ **Rewards:** A player who destroys all of their opponent's flag wins the game.

Iteration 1: Create the Single-Player Version

In this section, I show you how to make the single-player version of Capture the Flag. When you are making a multiplayer game, make a single-player version first, to ensure that the game mechanics (such as giving wands) are correct, before adding an extra layer of complexity (the second player).

Set up the player

1. Create a `main` function with a variable named `names`, as shown in Figure 8-6.

Figure 8-6

2. Set `names` to a list, as shown in Figure 8-7 and Figure 8-8.

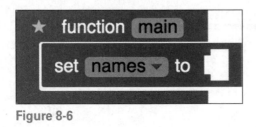

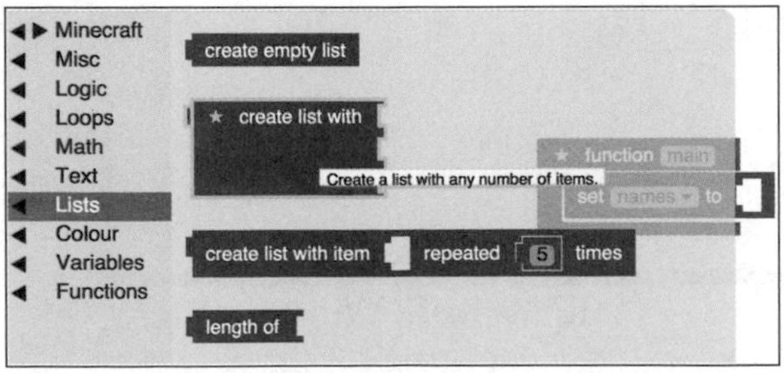

Figure 8-7

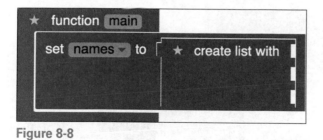

Figure 8-8

3. To start, you need 1 player, so click the star on the list, as shown in Figure 8-9.

Figure 8-9

4. Move the two extra items out of the list, as shown in Figure 8-10.

5. Place a text block in the empty item space, and type your Minecraft username, as shown in Figure 8-11.

6. Test the game. So far, you only know who the player is, so just print that info. Add a Send message block, as shown in Figure 8-12.

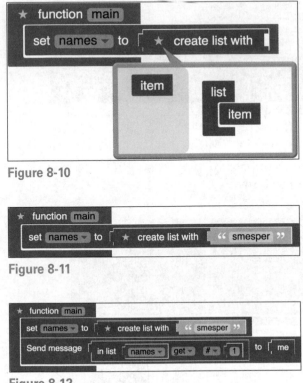

Figure 8-10

Figure 8-11

Figure 8-12

7. Test the game in Minecraft.

You see the scene shown in Figure 8-13.

Add a wand

In this section, I tell you how to add a wand item to the inventory. The wand doesn't *do* anything; it's simply an item with a new skin on it — a wand skin. In the section after this one, I tell you how to add magic to the wand.

Luckily, LearnToMod modding experts (the creators of LearnToMod) have designed new wands for you to use in the game. And, as in Project 7, you can import a library into your mod to use the wands without having to rewrite it all.

Figure 8-13

To add a wand to the inventory, follow these steps:

1. Import the Example Wand mod.

   The import can be found under the Misc category, as shown in Figure 8-14.

2. Type **examples-magic_wands** into the `import` block, as shown in Figure 8-15.

3. Create a new function named `SetupPlayer`, and move the `names` list into that function. Then call the `SetupPlayer` function from `main`, as shown in Figure 8-16.

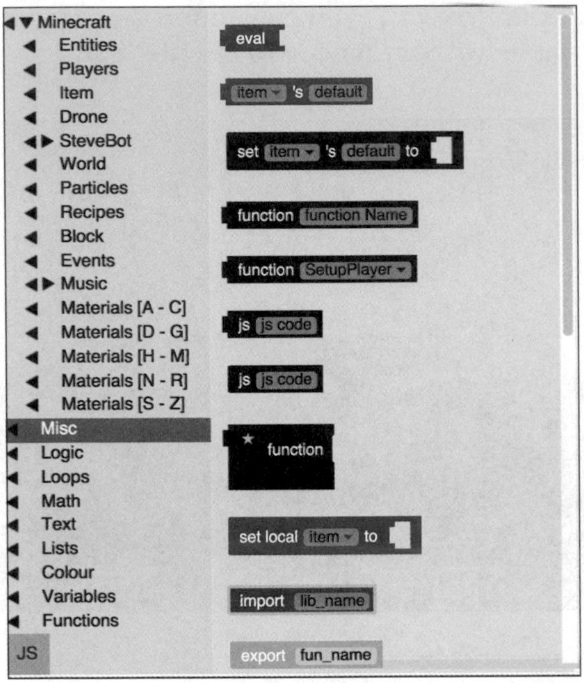

Figure 8-14

Figure 8-15

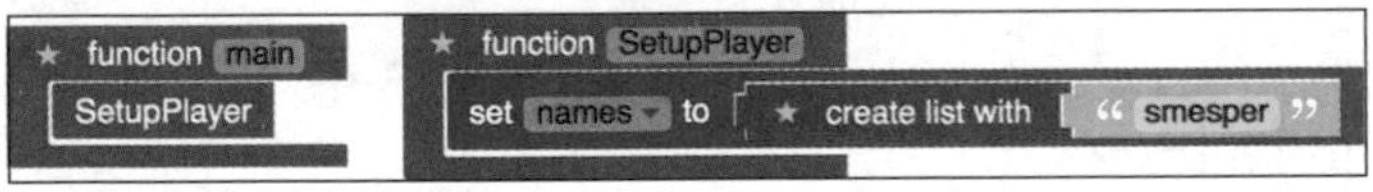

Figure 8-16

4. Under the Functions category, grab the `examples-magic_wands.init` function (as shown in Figure 8-17) and call it from `main`, as shown in Figure 8-18.

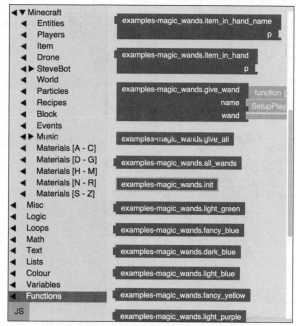

Figure 8-17

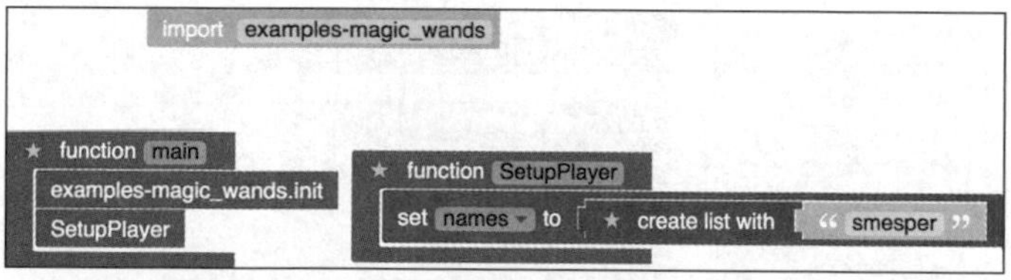

Figure 8-18

5. Under the Functions category, grab the examples-magic_wands.give_wand function (as shown in Figure 8-19) and the examples-magic_wands.light_green function (as shown in Figure 8-20).

6. Put the call to give_wand in the SetupPlayer function, where the name is a text block with ExplosionWand, and the wand is the light_green wand from Figure 8-20, just like in Figure 8-21.

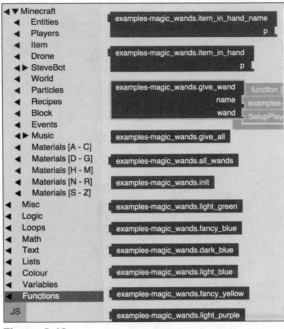

Figure 8-19

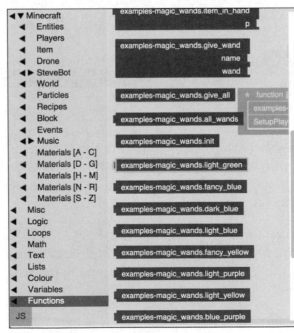

Figure 8-20

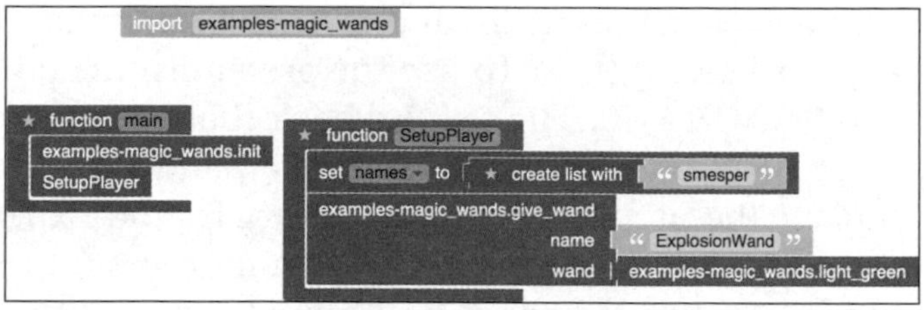

Figure 8-21

7. Test your mod in Minecraft.

When you run it, you see a message saying that a texture pack is being loaded. Then you see the green wand show up in the inventory, as shown in Figure 8-22. A *texture pack* is a change to the way objects look in Minecraft.

Figure 8-22

Awesome! Now it's time to see what actions the magic_wand functions are performing:

1. Go to mod.learntomod.com/programs/examples-magic_ wands to see all the code you're using.

2. The init function, as you can see in Figure 8-23, loads in the texture pack that the creators of LearnToMod have created for you!

Figure 8-23

The light_green function, as you can see in Figure 8-24, simply returns RECORD_10. In Minecraft, each material has an ID, such as 137, and the Discs that we are using to represent wands have IDs 3–12. To access them you must use the keyword RECORD. So, to use the green disc, you need access it with RECORD_10. The texture pack that you import in the init function is basically loading a picture of a wand to replace the picture of the disc. LearnToMod Experts created these wand pictures. You can learn more about this topic in the Magic Wands badges under the Learn category.

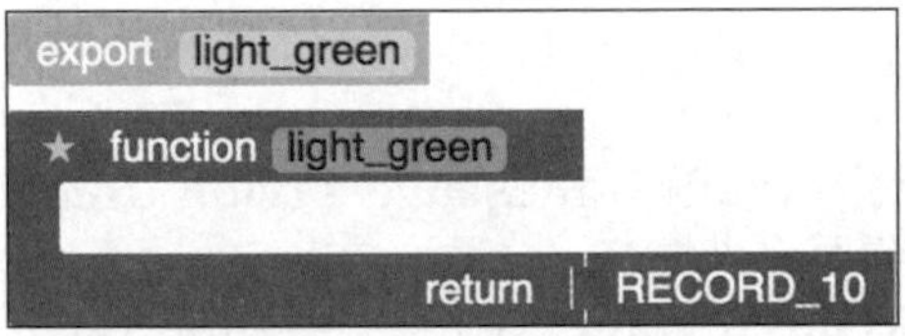

Figure 8-24

The give_wand function, as you can see in Figure 8-25, creates a new item with the material that you chose to pass as the parameter (light_green wand, in this case). Then it gives the item a name, the one that you pass as the parameter. Finally, it adds the item to the player's inventory.

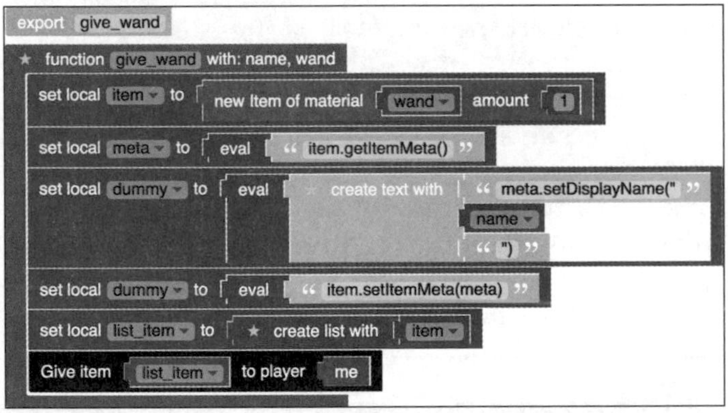

Figure 8-25

Prepare the wand for magic

In this section, you call a function when the player interacts with the magic wand. Follow these steps:

1. Create an event that calls a function when a `player_interact` event happens, as shown in Figure 8-26.

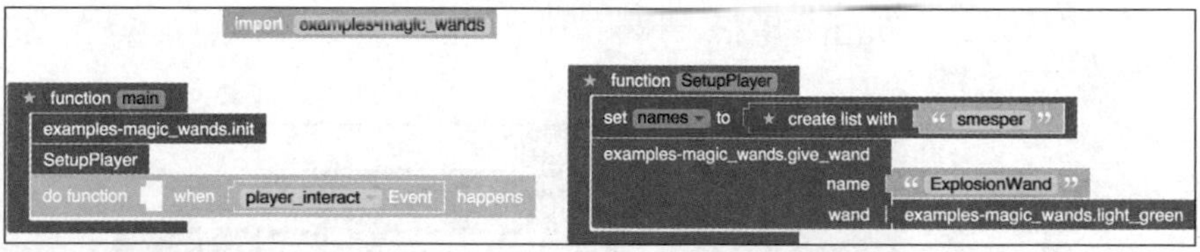

Figure 8-26

2. Then create a new function named `CastSpell`, which is called from the event.

   The only thing this function should do is send a message saying that the spell has been cast, as shown in Figure 8-27.

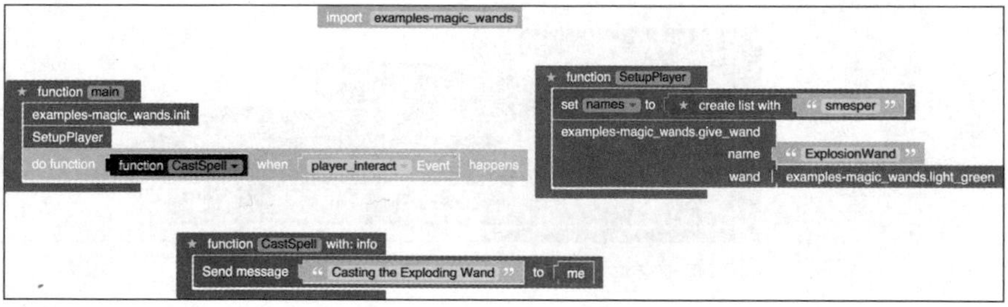

Figure 8-27

3. Test the mod.

   Notice that when you run the mod, a wand appears in the inventory (as it did in the previous section). Then when you try to use the wand, you see the message `Casting the Exploding Wand`.

The problem is that when you try to use *any* item, you see the message `Casting the Exploding Wand`. Try it!

To only associate the `CastSpell` function with the wand, follow these steps:

1. Identify which player caused the event and save that information in a local variable named `WandPlayer`, as shown in Figure 8-28.

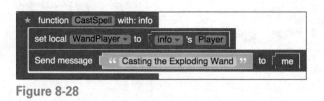

Figure 8-28

2. Get the name of the item in the player's hand by using the `magic_wands` library function `Get Item In Hand Name` function and passing the `WandPlayer` in as the parameter, as shown in Figure 8-29.

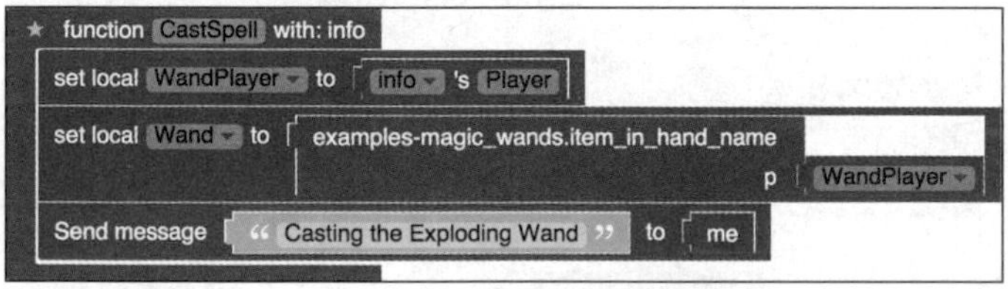

Figure 8-29

3. Check to see whether the item the player just interacted with was the exploding wand, and send the message only if that is the case, as shown in Figure 8-30.

4. Test the mod again.

   This time, the message appears only when you try to use the wand, but not any other item.

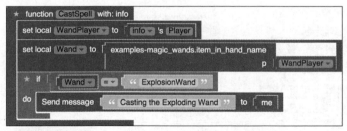

Figure 8-30

Design the wand's magic

After you have a wand and you know when the player is trying to use it, you can make the wand cast a spell!

The wand you made in the previous section is the explosion wand. In Project 7, you see how to make a mod that throws a block and causes an explosion when it lands. You reuse that code here. (You can see the code in Figure 8-31 and Figure 8-32.)

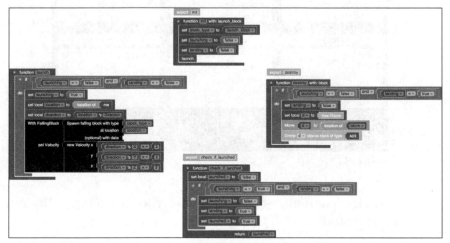

Figure 8-31

Before you make changes to the code, you should understand how all the mods you're using will interact. Figure 8-33 shows the three mods you should have at this point, if you have followed all the steps in this project so far: CaptureTheFlag, ExplodingProjectile, and ProjectileLibrary.

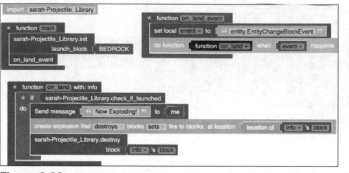

Figure 8-32

Capture The Flag	Exploding Projectile	Projectile Library
main	**main**	**init - launch_block**
init magic_wands	init Projectile Library	set variables
setup player	on_land_event	call launch
player interact -> Cast Spel		
SetupPlayer	**on_land_event**	**launch**
names["smesper"]	Event -> Change block	if OK to launch
Give Light Green Wand	Change Block	launch from
Called "Explosion Wand"	on_land	location of player
CastSpell	**on_land -info**	**check_if_launched**
WandPlayer	if launched (library)	Checks state
Wand	Send Message	
If "Explosion Wand"	Explosion	
Send Message	Destroy (library)	
Explosing Projectile		
		destroy - block
		Destroys block

Figure 8-33

Review each mod to be sure that you understand the purpose of each mod:

✔ CaptureTheFlag: In this mod, you know who the players are, and you know which wands you want to give each player. You need to be able to associate a certain type of wand (like ExplodingProjectile) with the wand, and you need to have the exploding projectile start from the player using the wand.

✔ ExplodingProjectile: The exploding projectile sends a message, which needs to go to the player who has cast the spell, not me, so a parameter needs to be passed into this mod.

✔ ProjectileLibrary: The projectile library needs to know from where to originate the projectile so that it doesn't always start at the location of me. A parameter needs to be passed to this mod as well.

Change the Projectile Library mod

You should start by changing the projectile library:

1. Add a parameter to the init function named casting_player, as shown in Figure 8-34.

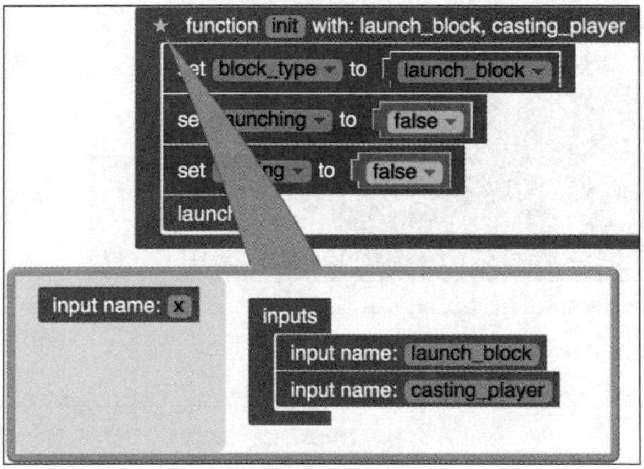

Figure 8-34

2. Create a new global variable named player, and set its value to casting_player, as shown in Figure 8-35.

3. In the launch function, change the location to become the location of the player, not me, as shown in Figure 8-36.

   Your mod should have the green Saved icon in the top-right corner of the programming environment.

At this point, the entire ProjectileLibrary mod should look like Figure 8-37.

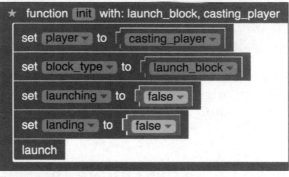

Figure 8-35

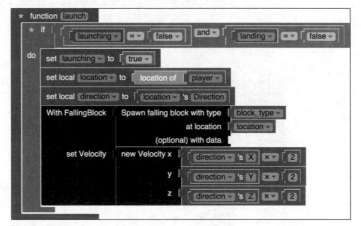

Figure 8-36

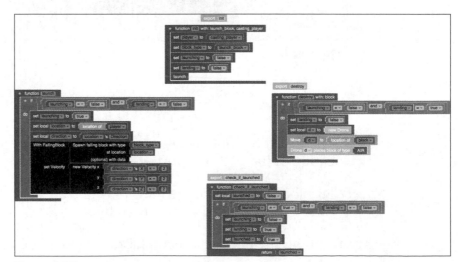

Figure 8-37

Change the Exploding Projectile mod

After your projectile library can be given the casting player, it's time to change the ExplodingProjectile mod to be able to accept the casting player, and pass it to the library:

1. Click in the import statement. Delete the last *y* in the word Library, and then and type it in again, see Figure 8-38.

   This step causes LearnToMod to update the library it's using.

   Figure 8-38

2. Now whenever you look at the functions that you can use from ProjectileLibrary, you will see the init function has a new parameter, casting_player, as shown in Figure 8-39.

3. Replace the call to ProjectileLibrary.init with the new function, as shown in Figure 8-40.

4. Add a parameter to main named casting_player, as shown in Figure 8-41.

5. Add a global variable named player that is set to the casting_player parameter, as shown in Figure 8-42.

6. In the on_land function, change the me block to player. Be sure to also delete and add back in the call to the check_if_launched and destroy functions.

   You have to delete the old ones and add the new ones back in because you updated the library. The on_land function now looks like Figure 8-43.

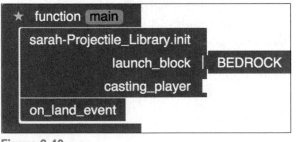

Figure 8-39

Figure 8-40

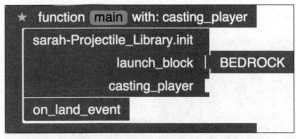

```
★  function  main  with: casting_player
   sarah-Projectile_Library.init
                    launch_block  |  BEDROCK
                    casting_player
   on_land_event
```

Figure 8-41

```
★  function  main  with: casting_player
   set  player ▼  to  [ casting_player ▼
   sarah-Projectile_Library.init
                    launch_block  |  BEDROCK
                    casting_player  |  player ▼
   on_land_event
```

Figure 8-42

```
★  function  on_land  with: info
★  if    sarah-Projectile_Library.check_if_launched
   do   Send message  " Now Exploding! "  to  [ player ▼
        create explosion that  destroys ▼  blocks  sets ▼  fire to blocks  at location  [ location of  [ info ▼ 's block
        sarah-Projectile_Library.destroy
                    block  |  [ info ▼ 's block
```

Figure 8-43

7. Change the main function to launch, and export the launch function, as shown in Figure 8-44.

At this point, the entire ExplodingProjectile mod looks like Figure 8-45.

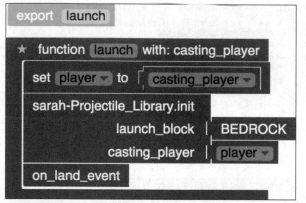

Figure 8-44

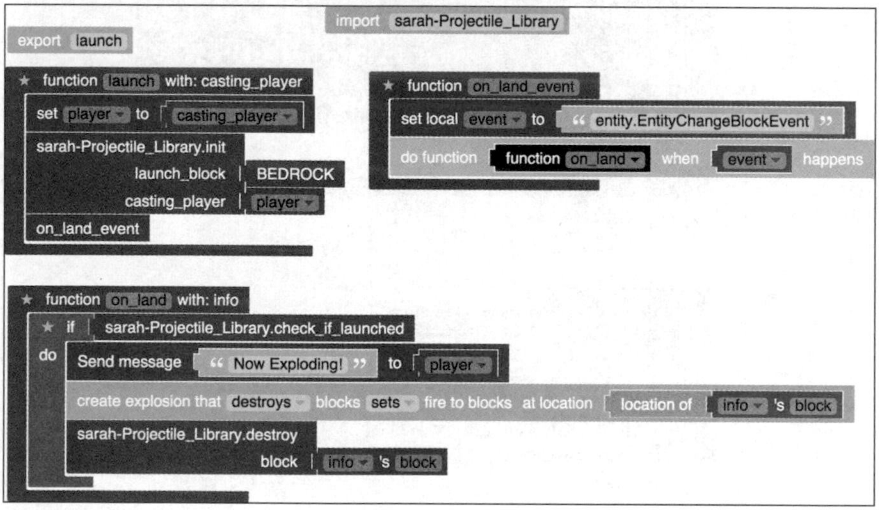

Figure 8-45

Make your wand use magic

After your old mods can handle who is casting the spell, you can call the launch mod from your CaptureTheFlag mod. Follow these steps:

1. Import the ExplodingProjectile library into your CaptureTheFlag mod, as shown in Figure 8-46.

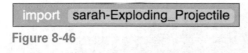

Figure 8-46

2. In the Functions category, drag the `Launch` function into the programming environment, as shown in Figure 8-47.

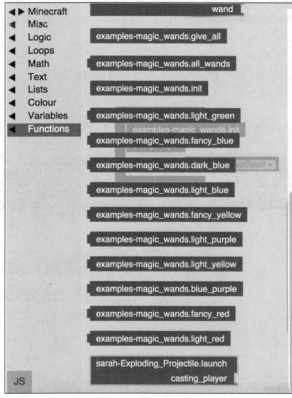

Figure 8-47

3. Add a call to the `launch` function in your CastSpell function, passing `WandPlayer` in as the `casting_player` parameter. Also, change the message to be sent to `WandPlayer`, as shown in Figure 8-48.

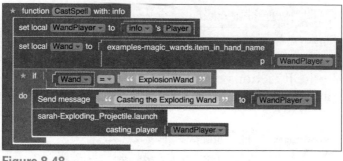

Figure 8-48

At this point, the entire `CaptureTheFlag` mod looks like Figure 8-49.

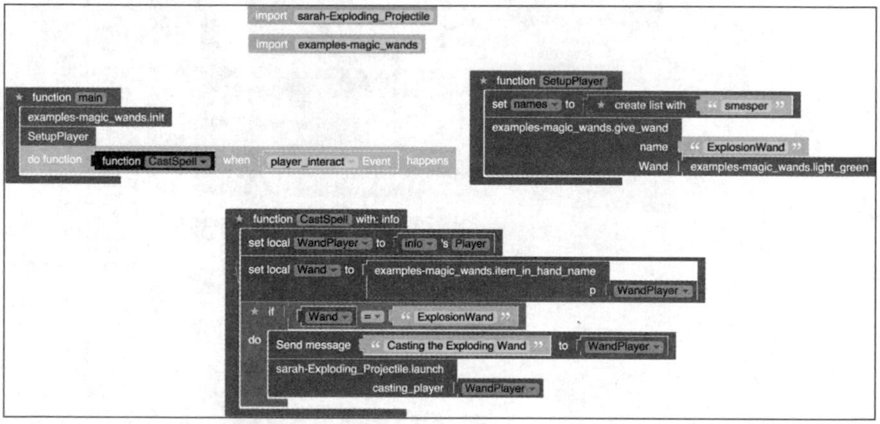

Figure 8-49

4. Test your mod.

This time, when you run the mod, you receive a light green wand. When you try to use the wand, a projectile is thrown; when it lands, it causes an explosion.

Give the player a flag

After the player has a wand that can cast magic, you should give her a flag to protect. Follow these steps:

1. Create a function called `give_flag` that takes 1 parameter named `flag_type`, as shown in Figure 8-50.

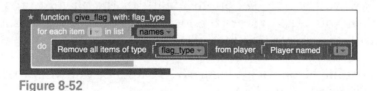

Figure 8-50

2. Use a counted loop to loop through all names in the `names` list, as shown in Figure 8-51.

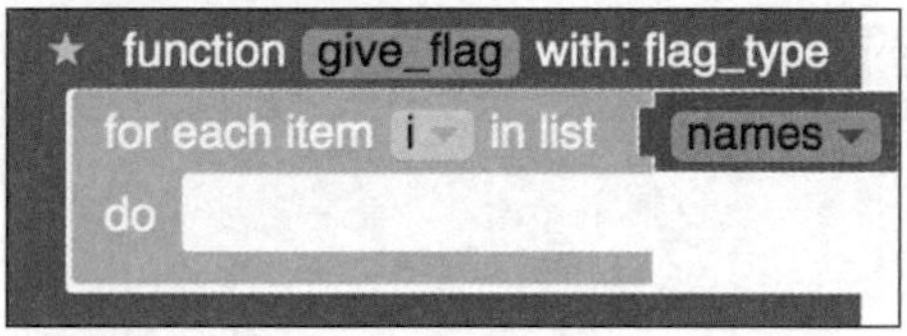

> ★ function **give_flag** with: flag_type
> > for each item **i** in list **names**
> > do

Figure 8-51

3. Remove all flags from the inventory of each player, as shown in Figure 8-52.

> ★ function **give_flag** with: flag_type
> > for each item **i** in list **names**
> > do Remove all items of type **flag_type** from player **Player named** **i**

Figure 8-52

4. Give each player in the list 1 item of type `flag_type`, as shown in Figure 8-53.

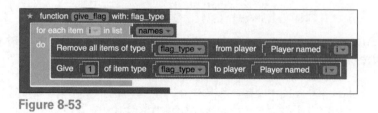

Figure 8-53

5. Call the new function from the `SetupPlayer` function, as shown in Figure 8-54.

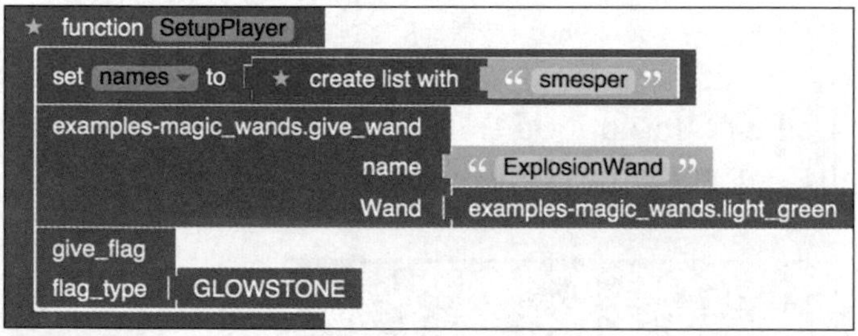

Figure 8-54

Test the mod.

Now you get a light green wand and one glowstone to place.

Store the player's flag locations

Now you need to set up the ability for the player to respawn at his flag. You need to store the location of the flags and associate that with the player that placed it.

This might be tricky. Figure 8-55 sketches out what to do, as explained in this list:

✔ `respawn_locations` is an object that holds other objects. The objects it holds are lists associated with names of players.

✔ "`smesper`" is the name of the first player, but that would mean I would have to be playing. Change it to be your Minecraft name.

✔ `players_respawn_list` is the list of respawn locations, and it should start out empty.

Figure 8-55

You should set up this object in the `give_flag` function. Follow these steps:

1. Create a new object named `respawn_locations`, as shown in Figure 8-56.

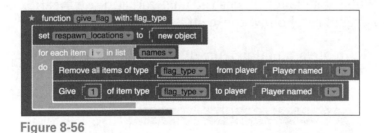

Figure 8-56

2. For each player, create an empty list named `players_respawn_locations`, as shown in Figure 8-57.

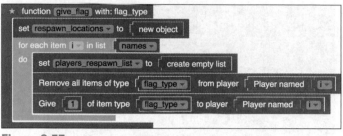

Figure 8-57

3. Place the empty list in the new object you just created, with the name of the player as the way to access the list, as shown in Figure 8-58.

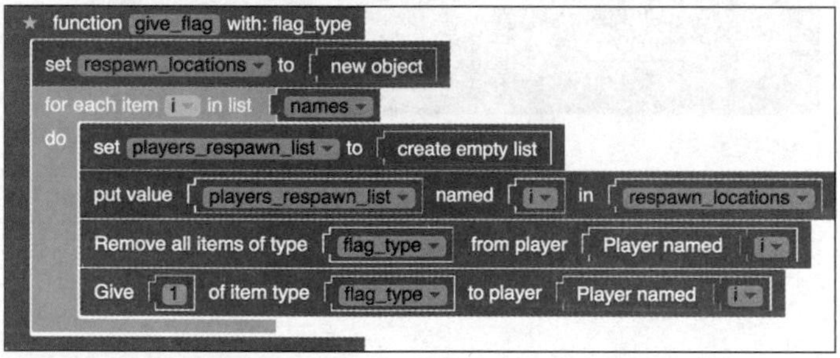

Figure 8-58

When the player places the flag, you add the location to her specific list. Follow these steps:

1. Create a function named `setup_respawn_locations` with the parameter `info`, as shown in Figure 8-59.

Figure 8-59

2. Call the `setup_respawn_locations` function from `main` when a `block_placed` event happens, as shown in Figure 8-60.

Figure 8-60

3. Create six new, local variables to gather the information about who placed what block, as shown in Figure 8-61.

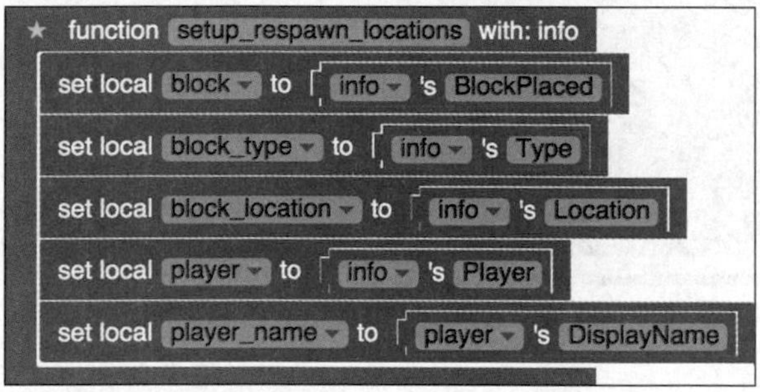

Figure 8-61

4. Check to see whether the block that was placed is a `flag_type` block, as shown in Figure 8-62.

5. Create a local variable named `player_respawn_list`, and get the actual list for the player who placed the block from the object you created in the `give_flag` function, as shown in Figure 8-63.

6. Check to see whether the list exists, as shown in Figure 8-64. If it doesn't, the player isn't one of the players in the game.

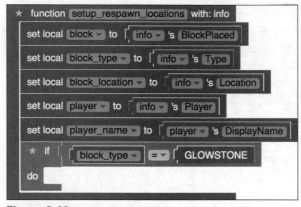

Figure 8-62

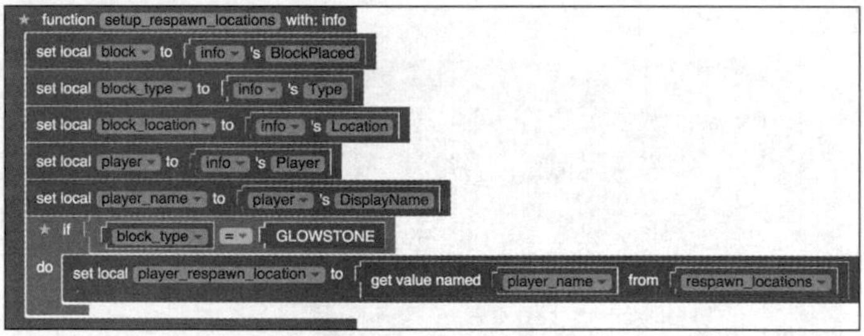

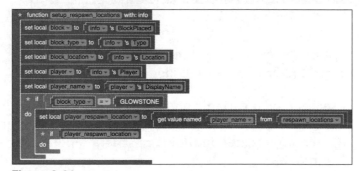

Figure 8-63

Figure 8-64

7. If the list exists, add the block's location to the list using JavaScript, as shown in Figure 8-65.

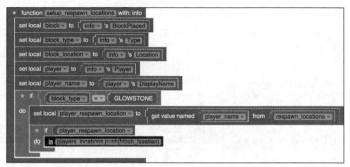

Figure 8-65

Respawn players at their flag locations

The final step to this iteration of the CaptureTheFlag Mod is to make the players respawn at their flag's location. Follow these steps:

1. Create a function named `respawn_player` with the parameter `info`, as shown in Figure 8-66.

Figure 8-66

2. Add a call to `respawn_player` when a `respawn_event` happens.

   Use the JavaScript block to do this, as shown in Figure 8-67.

Figure 8-67

3. Create three local variables to get the data from the `info` parameter and the list of respawn locations, as shown in Figure 8-68.

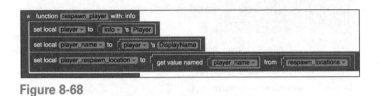

Figure 8-68

4. Check to see whether a respawn location exists for that player, as shown in Figure 8-69.

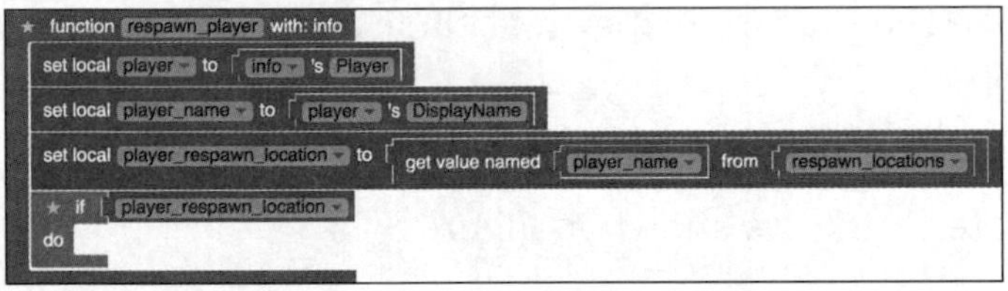

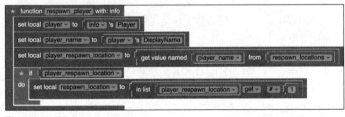

Figure 8-69

5. If a location exists, create a local variable to represent the location of the flag, as shown in Figure 8-70.

Figure 8-70

6. Two seconds (2000 milliseconds) after the player respawns, teleport her to the location of the flag, as shown in Figure 8-71.

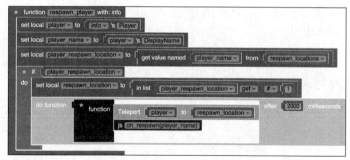

Figure 8-71

Test Iteration 1

Congratulations! You should have a pretty large mod at this point, and you can see all of its code in Figure 8-72.

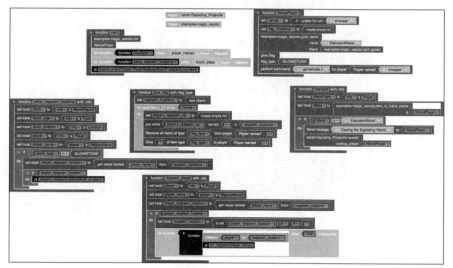

Figure 8-72

Now it's time to test the mod. When you run it, these three things happen:

✔ One glowstone and one light green magic wand are added to the inventory, and you go into Survival mode.

✔ When you use the magic wand, the exploding projectile gets created.

✔ Place the glowstone somewhere and then die. When you respawn, you're taken to your glowstone.

Make sure that your code is working before you move on to Project 9.

Iterating on Gameplay Using an Existing Game: Capture the Flag

In this project, I show you how to convert the single-player version of Capture the Flag to multiplayer. Playing Capture the Flag by yourself isn't much fun — you need to have at least one other player. Before reading this project, complete all the code instructions from Project 8. Your code example should look like Figure 8-73. Then test all the code you wrote in Project 8.

Always test the code before you start making changes.

First I show you how to change the gameplay loop to include the second player and how to iterate over the code to add the second player to each function. This ensures that the second

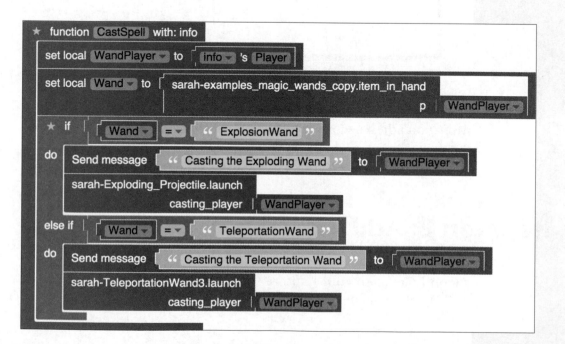

player is also getting a wand, getting respawn locations, and being able to respawn at the respawn location.

Look at the gameplay loop shown in Figure 9-1 (and defined in Project 8): It shows that you have completed all steps in the Start phase and you're facing a new challenge — adding Player 2 to the game.

Figure 9-1

After you add a second player, you need to add a way to beat the game. In this project, I walk you through the last two iterations of the gameplay loop: adding player two and making someone win.

Iteration 2: Add Player 2

In the following sections, I walk you through the steps to add a second player to your Capture the Flag game. The code you wrote in Project 8 was designed to make it easy to add players.

Add the new player to your list

To add a second player, you first have to add the person to the list of players in your code. Follow these steps:

1. Click on the star on the `names` list in the `SetupPlayer` function, as shown in Figure 9-2.

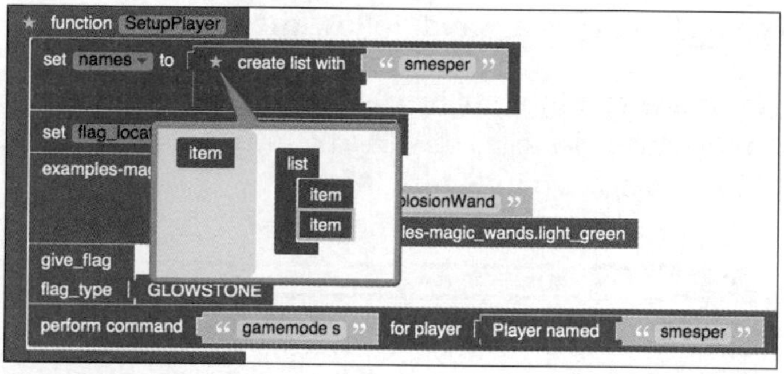

Figure 9-2

2. Add your friend's Minecraft username to the list, as shown in Figure 9-3.

   To avoid getting errors, spell your friend's Minecraft username correctly.

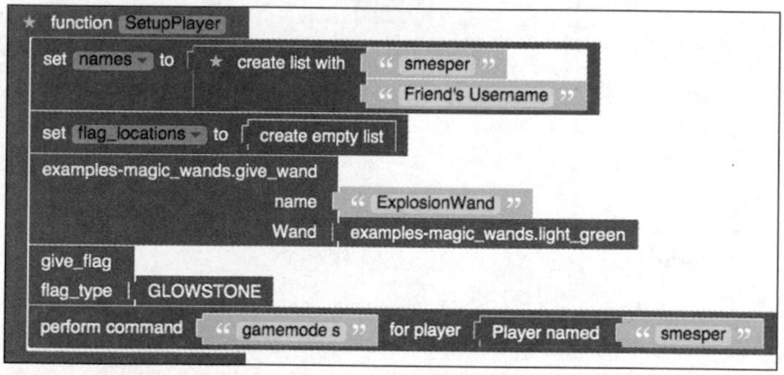

Figure 9-3

3. Put a loop around the player command block so that you're setting all players to Survival mode, as shown in Figure 9-4.

Figure 9-4

Give all players wands

To give all players a wand, follow these steps:

1. In a new tab in your browser, go to `mod.learntomod.com/programs/examples-magic_wands` and click Copy This Mod, as shown in Figure 9-5.

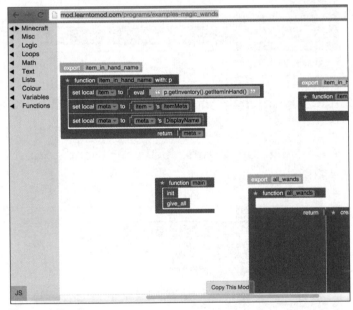

Figure 9-5

2. Go to: `mod.learntomod.com/book/mod` and click on the Examples Magic Wands mod, shown in Figure 9-6.

3. Click on the Code box in the lower-right corner, as shown in Figure 9-7.

   Now you can claim your own copy of the Magic Wands badge, and you can edit it to give wands to more than one person.

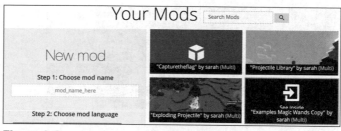

Figure 9-6

Figure 9-7

4. Add a new parameter named `player_names` to the `init` function, as shown in Figure 9-8.

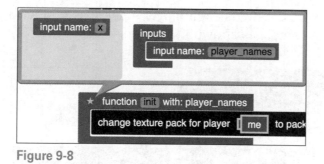

Figure 9-8

5. Create a global variable named `players`. *Global* variables are ones that all functions in the mod can see. They're the opposite of local variables (see Project 7).

It's a list of all players in the game (see Figure 9-9).

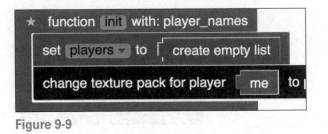

Figure 9-9

6. Add a loop around the texture pack change, shown in Figure 9-10.

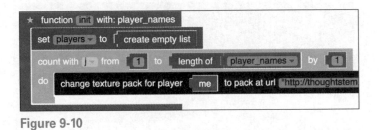

Figure 9-10

7. Create a local variable named player.

The variable holds each player's name as you loop through the list of names, as shown in Figure 9-11.

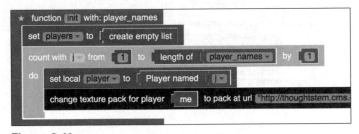

Figure 9-11

8. Add the player to the list of players you created in Step 5, as shown in Figure 9-12.

9. Replace the me block with the player block, as shown in Figure 9-13.

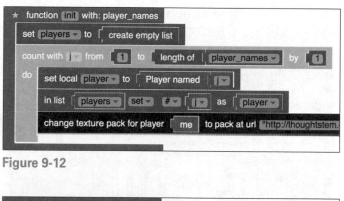

Figure 9-12

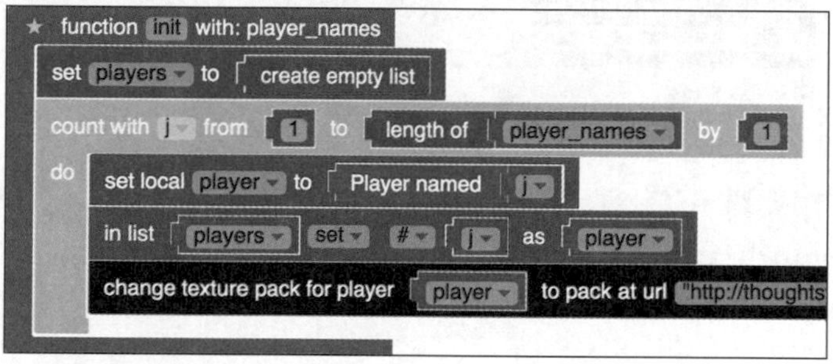

Figure 9-13

10. In the `give_wand` function, add a loop around the `give_item` block so that you can give the item to each player, as shown in Figure 9-14.

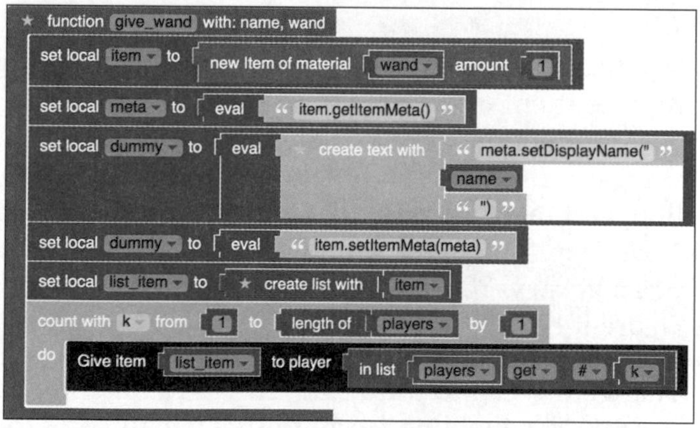

Figure 9-14

11. Do the same thing as in Step 10 for the `give_all` function, shown in Figure 9-15.

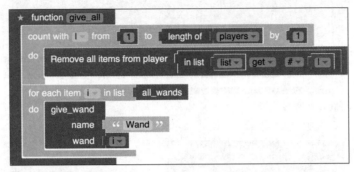

Figure 9-15

Import your own Magic Wands library

In your CaptureTheFlag mod, you need to import the Magic Wands library (the one that I show you how to change in the previous section).

1. Change the `import` statement to import *your* Magic Wands library, as shown in Figure 9-16.

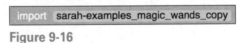

Figure 9-16

2. Delete all calls to the `example-magic_wands` functions, and replace them with the function calls to *your* `magic_wands` library functions, like you did in Project 8. Move the call to the `magic_wands.init` function to the `SetupPlayer` function, and make sure that your call to `give_wands` and the `light_green` wand is from your library, not from the `examples` library. Your `SetupPlayer` function should look like Figure 9-17.

3. Change the call to the `item_in_hand` function in the `CastSpell` function to your library instead of to the `examples` library, as shown in Figure 9-18.

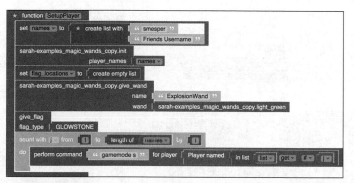

Figure 9-17

Figure 9-18

Test your game

At this point, your entire mod should be able to handle multiple players. CaptureTheFlag should look like Figure 9-19.

To test your game, invite a friend to join your server. Follow these steps:

1. On your LearnToMod private server, type **/open**.

   A message appears, showing your server number.

2. After your friend is on her own LearnToMod private server, have her type **/join ##**, where ## is the number of your server.

   After your friend has joined, find each other in the Minecraft world and run your mod. You should each get 1 light green mod and 1 glowstone flag.

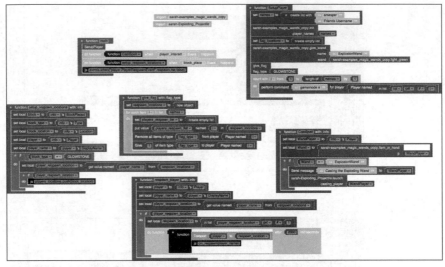

Figure 9-19

If one of you dies, you respawn to *your* glowstone block, not to your opponent's. Experiment!

Iteration 3: Make Someone Win

The final iteration I describe in this project is how to announce when someone loses. To lose, the player must die and not have a flag to spawn back to. The goal of the game, then, is to destroy your opponent's flag so that he cannot respawn. In Minecraft, you can't capture anything without destroying it, so maybe we should have named this mod DestroyTheFlag.

The only changes you need to make are to the `respawn_player` function. Follow these steps:

1. Add a loop that loops through all of the players' `respawn_locations`, and remove the data that you were originally setting to the `respawn_location` variable.

   The function looks like Figure 9-20.

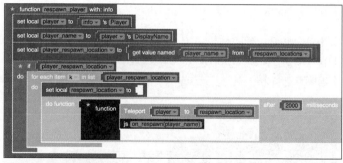

Figure 9-20

2. Set the `respawn_location` variable to the variable *k,* which is one of the respawn locations for the player who is respawning, as shown in Figure 9-21.

Figure 9-21

3. Create a local variable named `block`, which is the block that's at the location of the respawn location, as shown in Figure 9-22.

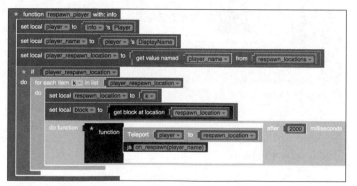

Figure 9-22

4. Check to see whether the block at that location is glowstone.

   If it is glowstone, the flag is still there; if it isn't glowstone, the opponent has destroyed the flag. The function looks like Figure 9-23.

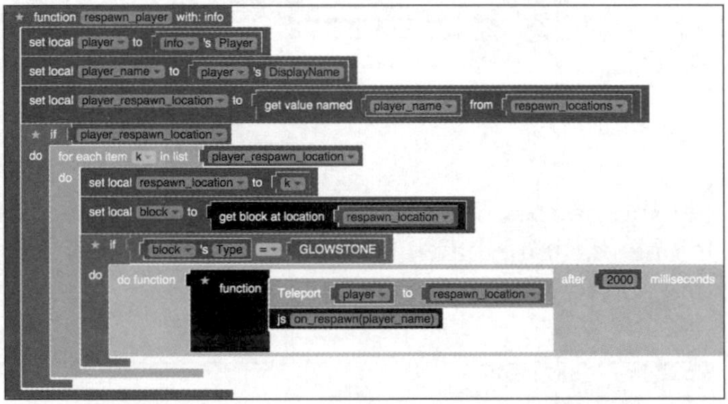

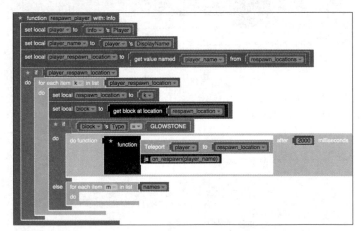

Figure 9-23

5. If the flag is no longer there, loop through all players in the game, as shown in Figure 9-24.

Figure 9-24

6. Send a message to everyone saying that the player has lost, as shown in Figure 9-25.

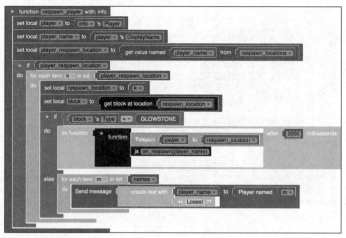

Figure 9-25

Whew — now you have a multiplayer Capture the Flag game!

Make the game your own

Using the powerful Capture the Flag game described in this project, you can continue iterating on the gameplay loop. Here are some ideas on how to enhance the game:

✔ Add flags for each player.

✔ Add new kinds of wands for each player.

✔ Give each player different wands.

What are your ideas? Be sure to share them on the LearnToMod forums at forum.learntomod.com.

Give players teleportation wands

After you have tested your game, edit your code to give each player a teleportation wand:

1. Add a second call to the give_wand function inside the SetupPlayer function, as shown in Figure 9-26.

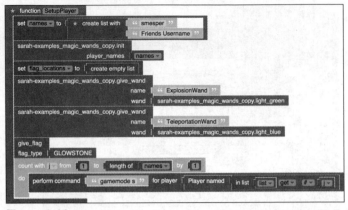

Figure 9-26

2. In the `CastSpell` function, click on the star on the `if` statement and add an `else-if` statement, as shown in Figure 9-27.

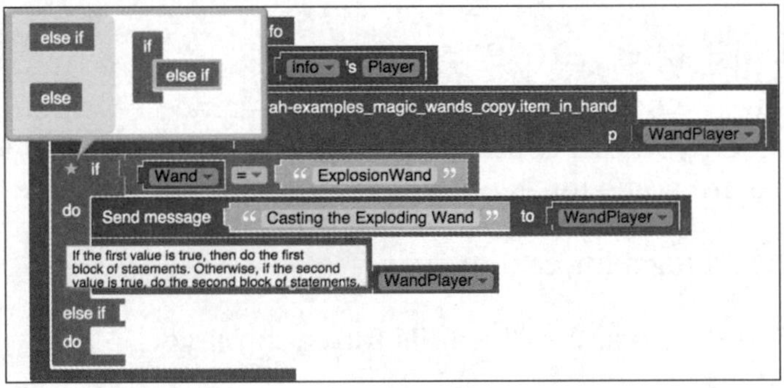

Figure 9-27

3. Compare `Wand` with `TeleportationWand` so that you can call the teleportation function *only* if the `TeleportationWand` was used, as shown in Figure 9-28.

4. Go to the Exploding Projectile mod and make a copy of it. Open the copied mod and rename it **TeleportationWand**. Then import `TeleportationWand` to your `CaptureTheFlag` mod, as shown in Figure 9-29.

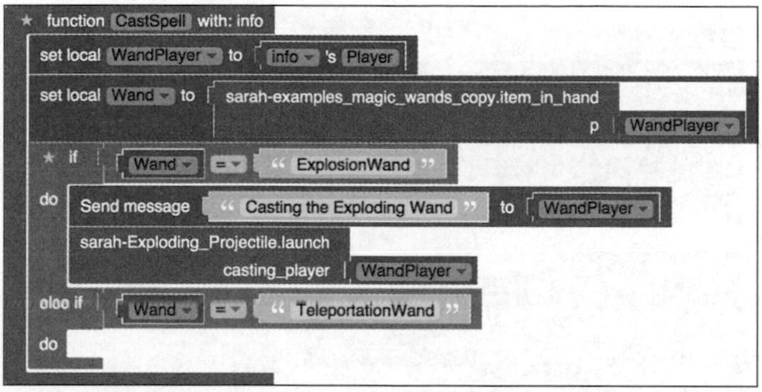

Figure 9-28

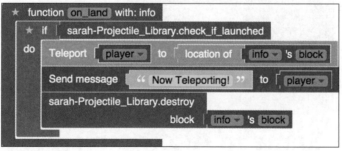

Figure 9-29

5. Change the on_land function in the Teleportation Wand mod to teleport the player rather than explode the block, as shown in Figure 9-30.

Figure 9-30

6. The entire Teleportation Wand mod looks like the one shown in Figure 9-31.

7. Call the launch function from the CastSpell function, and send a message that you're teleporting the player, as shown in Figure 9-32.

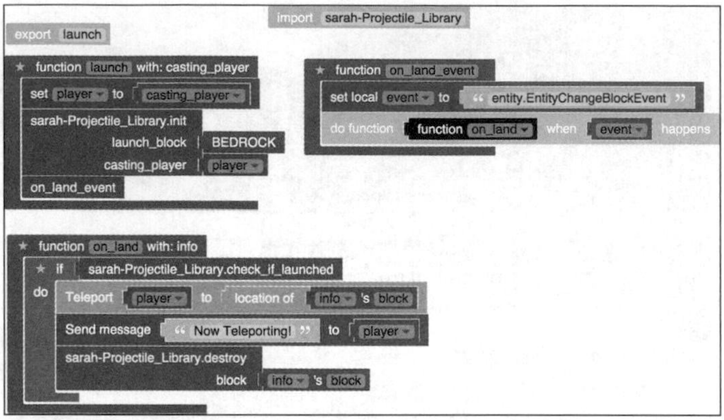

Figure 9-31

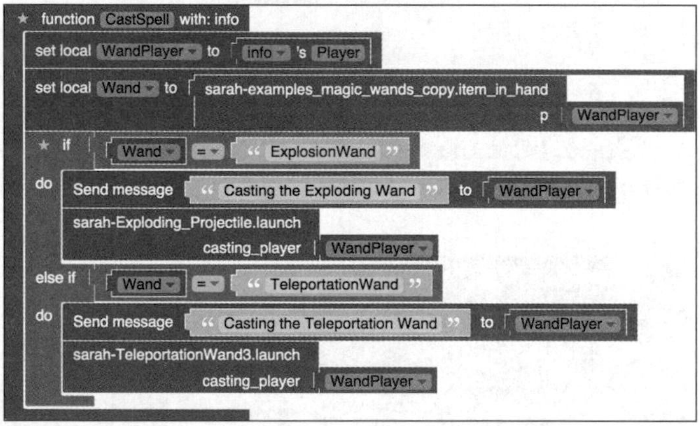

Figure 9-32

Play the Game in Alternative Ways

Here are some alternative ways to play the game of Capture the Flag:

✔ **Create a smaller arena.** Rather than hide glowstone flags in the infinite world of Minecraft, create a smaller arena to play in so that you face a new challenge.

✔ **Add the rules of Spleef (see Project 4) to your game with an arena.** This method makes it more likely that you'll die — even without your opponent attacking, because you could simply fall through the floor.

✔ **Set a timer.** Set one timer to limit how much time you can take to hide flags, and then set another timer to limit how long you have to find the glowstone flags.

What are *your* ideas for playing? Be sure to share them on the LearnToMod forums at `forum.learntomod.com`.

Part 4

Building Your Own Minecraft Minigame

This week you'll build:

Building Your
Own Game

Throughout this book, I describe lots of coding concepts
and game design strategies. In this project, however, I guide
you through the steps to create your own Minecraft mod. It's
time to put your new skills to use in a new and creative project
that you come up with on your own.

Coming up with new mod ideas can be a fun process all on its
own. Get together with friends and ask them what they wish
they could do in Minecraft, or watch YouTube videos for
inspiration.

Sketch Out Your Mod

The first thing to do when designing a new mod is to sketch out the result you want. Keep these guidelines in mind when you're sketching out your mod:

✔ **Use graph paper.** You can sketch out your mod more accurately on graph paper than on blank paper. Figure 10-1 shows what graph paper looks like. You can look at each box on the graph paper as a single block in Minecraft.

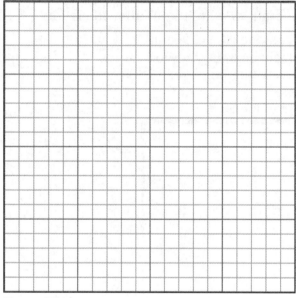

Figure 10-1

✔ **Math blocks can be even more useful than graph paper.** You can create the 3D effect, where you almost feel like you're walking around in the mod you're designing.

✔ **Using blank paper has its place, too.** Sometimes you just want to get a general idea of what your mod will look like or what it will do, so you don't need to add lots of detail.

✔ **Build it in Minecraft first.** If you're designing a mod in which you build a structure such as a roller coaster, build the structure by hand in Minecraft first, to form an idea of its construction.

✔ **Keep paper and a pencil handy.** Even after you sketch out your mod, you may need to jot down ideas or work through a problem in your mod.

Plan Your Mod

After you sketch your mod, you can plan which functions you need, such as one for setting up the mod's scene. You don't have to be precisely correct, but you should at least have an idea of what functions you will have.

Here are a few suggestions for planning your mod:

✔ Draw circles around structures, or even parts of structures, and name them.

✔ For parts of your mod that aren't structures, like events, draw a box with the following parts in it:

  • **At the top:** The name of the function

  • **Inside the box:** A list of actions the function should perform

✔ Ask yourself how data will be passed around your functions. Will it have parameters? Which variables should be local, and which should be global (see Project 7)?

After you have an understanding of the code you want to write, you can head to the LearnToMod site and start outlining, as described later in this project, in the section "Outline Your Mod."

Draw the Gameplay Loop

If you're making a minigame, remember to draw the gameplay loop, described fully in Project 4. You can use the drawing in Figure 10-2 as a template for the gameplay loop.

Figure 10-2

Here are some strategies for planning the gameplay loop:

- **Make a separate drawing for each iteration of the loop.** That way, you know how much you need to get done before you have a game that you can play.

- **Each iteration should result in a game that you can play.** It may not be a lot of fun in the first iteration, but it's still a game.

- **Feel free to change your mind.** If you think you have three iterations and the third one seems easier to complete than the second one, just swap them around.

The gameplay loop can be used in other situations too, as a general guideline, but it is most effective when you have a challenge — a goal you're trying to reach when you're playing in the mod that you made.

Outline Your Mod

After you understand the structure of your mod and how you want to approach breaking it up into functions, you can outline it in LearnToMod.

Follow these steps:

1. Go to `mod.learntomod.com` and click on Mod at the top of the screen.

2. Create a new mod and choose Blockly (Multiplayer) as the language.

3. Click the Code button to go to the coding environment.

4. Create all the functions that you outlined earlier, in the "Plan Your Mod" section, but don't fill them in yet.

   Just let the functions sit in your mod, empty, with names and parameters.

   Though these functions may end up changing as you iterate over your gameplay loop, it's important to start piecing together the code early on so that you don't miss any crucial actions.

5. Call the functions from the other functions as you think you would need to. For example: You will have a main function, and it might be that the `main` function calls all the other functions. If that is the case, put a call to each function inside of `main`.

This step list helps you visualize your code!

Refactor Your Mods

A mod that starts to grow too big for you to remember it all can cause a lot of problems because if you try to make changes, you might make changes in the wrong function.

Always consider refactoring your mods when they become too large to understand easily.

An effective way to refactor your mod is to turn it into a library and then import it into a new mod, where you have more control. I show you how to do this in Project 7 with the projectile library.

Another form of refactoring occurs when you simply change how your functions interact, or even which functions you have.

Before starting to refactor, save a copy of your mod so that you can always return to a working version.

Sometimes, when you're making simple refactoring changes, you can break your code. Be sure to continually test your code as you build it.

Test Your Code

Test, and test often. Avoid the situation where you spend hours writing code that doesn't even work and then have to rewrite it. That's when designing on paper and using a gameplay loop are helpful.

If you always have code that can be tested and you make only small changes between testing periods, you're more likely to create correct, working code that you can be proud of.

Share Your Mod with Friends

One of the best parts about writing mods in LearnToMod is that you can share them with friends. Anyone with a LearnToMod account can not only see the code you have written but also remix it! Account holders can make a copy of your mod, try it out, and even modify their own versions.

For the best way to share your mod, follow these steps:

1. Name it something awesome, such as Exploding Rollercoaster.

2. As I've done in Figure 10-3, add a screen shot (on the left side of the figure) and a description (on the right) to its page.

3. Publish it to the public mods, such as the ones at `mod.learntomod.com/program_profiles`.

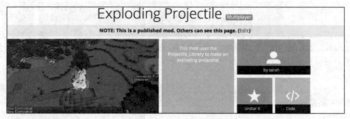

Figure 10-3

You can even invite your friends into your Minecraft private server so that you can show them the effects of your mods and chat with them about your experience.

Remix Other People's Mods

Just as you share your own mods, you should check out what other people have made, too.

On your home page, click on the Find a Mod button, as shown in Figure 10-4.

Thousands of people from around the world are sharing their mods every day. Some of them are shown in Figure 10-5.

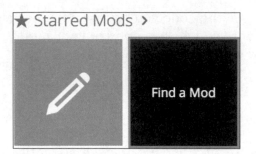

Figure 10-4

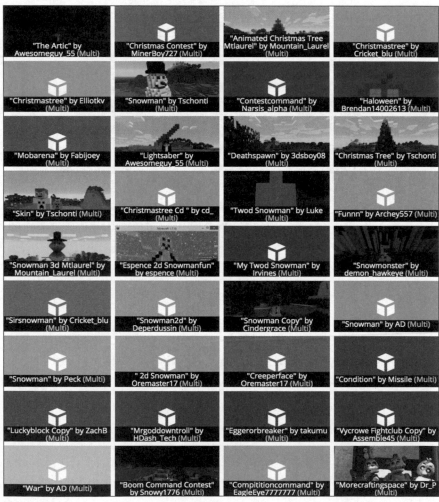

Figure 10-5

Browse the list of mods, and click on a mod that you find interesting. You can read its description to find out more and then click the Code button to make a copy of it in your own LearnToMod account.

An extra challenge for you is to try to figure out how to add something neat to a mod that someone else has made. Follow these steps:

1. Test the mod to see what it does, and compare that to what it is supposed to do.

2. Read the code, and draw it out. (It's sort of the reverse step of designing code.)

3. Design one addition to the code and figure out where it should go (for example, in its own function or inside another function).

4. As you add code, *test, test, test!*

After you have remixed the mod, share it with everyone else on the LearnToMod site to see how other coders can take it even further.

Engage with Your Community

If you've followed along with my instructions throughout this book, you're now a LearnToMod Minecraft modder! And a large community of coders are out there to learn from and share with — people who love to mod, just like you do. If you get stuck and can't figure out a coding problem, visit the LearnToMod forums and ask questions. You might even find that you can answer questions for other people.

Never hesitate to ask questions. One helpful way to learn is to fail without fear so that you can learn from your mistakes.

Index

About the Author

Sarah Guthals, Ph.D, is a computer scientist and an educator who has worked as a programmer at Microsoft, NASA-JPL, and ViaSat. She has also taught hundreds of teachers from around the world how to teach computer science to students as young as 7. Sarah is now the chief technical officer (CTO) and cofounder of ThoughtSTEM, where she develops curriculum and training for teaching computer science through Minecraft modding.

Stephen Foster, Ph.D, is an educator and software engineer who has been developing educational software for teaching coding throughout his career. Stephen is the CEO of ThoughtSTEM and acts as Lead Developer for ThoughtSTEM's educational technologies, which include LearnToMod and CodeSpells. Stephen paved the way for teaching kids coding through modding Minecraft.

Lindsey Handley, Ph.D, is a scientist and educator with a passion for high quality STEM education for K-12 students. Lindsey is currently the COO of ThoughtSTEM and manages its coding after-school programs and camps in over 25 locations across San Diego. Lindsey also provides support to teachers across the world who want to teach coding in their classrooms using the LearnToMod software.

Dedication

We dedicate this book to our close friends, and to our families, who have supported us not only in writing this book but also in becoming who we are today. We specifically dedicate this book to Adrian Guthals, who stayed up late at night to battle Sarah in Spleef, Monster Arena, and Capture the Flag. Those games wouldn't have been much fun if Adrian hadn't been there to play-test them.

Authors' Acknowledgments

We would like to acknowledge all of the hard work that went into making Minecraft, an incredibly fun and open-ended game played by millions around the world. Without Minecraft, we couldn't have made LearnToMod, and we couldn't have written this book. We also want to thank the hard-working coders who helped with LearnToMod — using their fast and creative problem-solving skills, we can help teach kids how to make even more with Minecraft. And, of course, we want to thank the millions of kids around the world who play Minecraft. *You* inspired us to teach coding through Minecraft!

Publisher's Acknowledgments

Acquisitions Editor: Amy Fandrei

Project Manager: Colleen Diamond

Development Editor: Becky Whitney

Copy Editor: Becky Whitney

Technical Editor: Nick Falkner, Ph.D

Editorial Assistant: Claire Brock

Sr. Editorial Assistant: Cherie Case

Production Editor: Suresh Srinivasan

Project Manager: Colleen Diamond

le & Mac

d For Dummies,
Edition
-1-118-72306-7

one For Dummies,
Edition
-1-118-69083-3

s All-in-One
Dummies, 4th Edition
-1-118-82210-4

X Mavericks
Dummies
3-1-118-69188-5

gging & Social Media

ebook For Dummies,
Edition
3-1-118-63312-0

ial Media Engagement
Dummies
3-1-118-53019-1

rdPress For Dummies,
Edition
3-1-118-79161-5

siness

ck Investing
Dummies, 4th Edition
8-1-118-37678-2

vesting For Dummies,
Edition
8-0-470-90545-6

Personal Finance
For Dummies, 7th Edition
978-1-118-11785-9

QuickBooks 2014
For Dummies
978-1-118-72005-9

Small Business Marketing
Kit For Dummies,
3rd Edition
978-1-118-31183-7

Careers

Job Interviews
For Dummies, 4th Edition
978-1-118-11290-8

Job Searching with Social
Media For Dummies,
2nd Edition
978-1-118-67856-5

Personal Branding
For Dummies
978-1-118-11792-7

Resumes For Dummies,
6th Edition
978-0-470-87361-8

Starting an Etsy Business
For Dummies, 2nd Edition
978-1-118-59024-9

Diet & Nutrition

Belly Fat Diet For Dummies
978-1-118-34585-6

Mediterranean Diet
For Dummies
978-1-118-71525-3

Nutrition For Dummies,
5th Edition
978-0-470-93231-5

Digital Photography

Digital SLR Photography
All-in-One For Dummies,
2nd Edition
978-1-118-59082-9

Digital SLR Video &
Filmmaking For Dummies
978-1-118-36598-4

Photoshop Elements 12
For Dummies
978-1-118-72714-0

Gardening

Herb Gardening
For Dummies, 2nd Edition
978-0-470-61778-6

Gardening with Free-Range
Chickens For Dummies
978-1-118-54754-0

Health

Boosting Your Immunity
For Dummies
978-1-118-40200-9

Diabetes For Dummies,
4th Edition
978-1-118-29447-5

Living Paleo For Dummies
978-1-118-29405-5

Big Data

Big Data For Dummies
978-1-118-50422-2

Data Visualization
For Dummies
978-1-118-50289-1

Hadoop For Dummies
978-1-118-60755-8

**Language &
Foreign Language**

500 Spanish Verbs
For Dummies
978-1-118-02382-2

English Grammar
For Dummies, 2nd Edition
978-0-470-54664-2

French All-in-One
For Dummies
978-1-118-22815-9

German Essentials
For Dummies
978-1-118-18422-6

Italian For Dummies,
2nd Edition
978-1-118-00465-4

𝑒 Available in print and e-book formats.

Available wherever books are sold. **For more information or to order direct visit www.dummies.com**

Math & Science

Algebra I For Dummies,
2nd Edition
978-0-470-55964-2

Anatomy and Physiology
For Dummies, 2nd Edition
978-0-470-92326-9

Astronomy For Dummies,
3rd Edition
978-1-118-37697-3

Biology For Dummies,
2nd Edition
978-0-470-59875-7

Chemistry For Dummies,
2nd Edition
978-1-118-00730-3

1001 Algebra II Practice
Problems For Dummies
978-1-118-44662-1

Microsoft Office

Excel 2013 For Dummies
978-1-118-51012-4

Office 2013 All-in-One
For Dummies
978-1-118-51636-2

PowerPoint 2013
For Dummies
978-1-118-50253-2

Word 2013 For Dummies
978-1-118-49123-2

Music

Blues Harmonica
For Dummies
978-1-118-25269-7

Guitar For Dummies,
3rd Edition
978-1-118-11554-1

iPod & iTunes
For Dummies, 10th Edition
978-1-118-50864-0

Programming

Beginning Programming
with C For Dummies
978-1-118-73763-7

Excel VBA Programming
For Dummies, 3rd Edition
978-1-118-49037-2

Java For Dummies,
6th Edition
978-1-118-40780-6

Religion & Inspiration

The Bible For Dummies
978-0-7645-5296-0

Buddhism For Dummies,
2nd Edition
978-1-118-02379-2

Catholicism For Dummies,
2nd Edition
978-1-118-07778-8

Self-Help & Relationships

Beating Sugar Addiction
For Dummies
978-1-118-54645-1

Meditation For Dummies,
3rd Edition
978-1-118-29144-3

Seniors

Laptops For Seniors
For Dummies, 3rd Edition
978-1-118-71105-7

Computers For Seniors
For Dummies, 3rd Edition
978-1-118-11553-4

iPad For Seniors
For Dummies, 6th Edition
978-1-118-72826-0

Social Security
For Dummies
978-1-118-20573-0

Smartphones & Tablets

Android Phones
For Dummies, 2nd Edition
978-1-118-72030-1

Nexus Tablets
For Dummies
978-1-118-77243-0

Samsung Galaxy S 4
For Dummies
978-1-118-64222-1

Samsung Galaxy Tabs
For Dummies
978-1-118-77294-2

Test Prep

ACT For Dummies,
5th Edition
978-1-118-01259-8

ASVAB For Dummies,
3rd Edition
978-0-470-63760-9

GRE For Dummies,
7th Edition
978-0-470-88921-3

Officer Candidate Tests
For Dummies
978-0-470-59876-4

Physician's Assistant Exam
For Dummies
978-1-118-11556-5

Series 7 Exam For Dummies
978-0-470-09932-2

Windows 8

Windows 8.1 All-in-One
For Dummies
978-1-118-82087-2

Windows 8.1 For Dummies
978-1-118-82121-3

Windows 8.1 For Dummies
Book + DVD Bundle
978-1-118-82107-7

Available in print and e-book formats.

Available wherever books are sold. **For more information or to order direct visit www.dummies.com**

Take Dummies with you everywhere you go!

Whether you are excited about e-books, want more from the web, must have your mobile apps, or are swept up in social media, Dummies makes everything easier.

Leverage the Power

For Dummies is the global leader in the reference category and one of the most trusted and highly regarded brands in the world. No longer just focused on books, customers now have access to the For Dummies content they need in the format they want. Let us help you develop a solution that will fit your brand and help you connect with your customers.

Advertising & Sponsorships

Connect with an engaged audience on a powerful multimedia site, and position your message alongside expert how-to content.

Targeted ads • Video • Email marketing • Microsites • Sweepstakes sponsorship